BRAD AND ADAM SERIES BOOK 1

What's your Financial Game Plan?

Neala Okuromade

www.bradandadamseries.com

First published in Great Britain in 2012 by Brad & Adam Publishing,
Suite O0003, 35 Victoria Road, Darlington, Co Durham, DL1 5SF
www.bradandadamseries.com

ISBN: 978-0-9575045-0-9

This publication is designed to educate and provide general information regarding the subject matter covered. Because each factual situation is different, specific advice should be tailored to the particular circumstances. You should consult with a professional where appropriate.

The author and publisher have taken reasonable precautions in the preparation of this book and believe the facts presented in the book are accurate as of the date it was written. However, the author and publisher assume no responsibility for any errors or omissions. The author and publisher specifically disclaim any liability resulting from the use or application of the information contained in this book, and the information is not intended to serve as legal advice to individual situations.

The author and publisher recommend that you use this publication in conjunction with other trusted sources and information.

A CIP record for this work can be obtained from the British Library.

Printed and bound in the UK by   Direct POD, part of Lonsdale Direct Solutions Ltd, Denington Estate, Wellingborough, NN8 2RA

Illustrations: Anna Hancock, www.annahancock.com

Cover: Emmantech Creative Solutions, www.emmantech.com

Editor and Typesetter: Claire Handy of Handy Editorials, www.handyeditorials.co.uk

Back cover photograph: © Stephen Hudson of ISOO Portrait www.isoo.co.uk

Dedication

To my wonderful, prudent mum. Thank you for teaching me sound financial principles. It has been an invaluable lesson that has held me in great stead. This book is for you.

About the Author:

Neala Okuromade, FCCA, was born in Trinidad and Tobago. She came to England to study accounting when she was 21, and decided to make it her home. Neala has over fourteen years' experience in accounting, including managing Finance departments. Her experience includes: Project Accountant for a large Property Company, where she supervised a multi-million pound project setting up the finance systems and procedures; a Financial Controller of a Property Exchange Service Company, which was later bought out by an American Nasdaq listed company; and the Associate Director of Finance for one of the fastest growing charities in England and Wales at the time. As well as managing company finances, she has also given one-on-one financial sessions to individuals needing budgeting and money management advice. She has counselled people on debt management and helped many of these individuals come out of debt and handle their money more effectively.

Neala is passionate about empowering the everyday person to make a success of their personal finances, especially in today's tough and chaotic economic climate. An avid studier for many years of world financial news, economics and investing, Neala now wants to take what she has studied, learnt and practiced, and simplify it for anyone who thinks anything financial is too complicated and impossible to understand.

Table of Contents

CONTENTS

Acknowledgements

I am indebted to my husband for his time, patience and belief in me when writing this book, even putting up with me constantly talking about 'Brad and Adam'. Michael, thank you

To my editor, Claire Handy, for her patience, perseverance and for making this book possible. You have been instrumental in this whole process, not just with your editing and suggestions but also in holding my hands through the really difficult periods and putting up with my highs and lows. I am grateful. I know you really believe in this book.

For all my proofreaders Emily, Sharon, Belinda and Awo, thank you for your time, effort and advice; it was very useful and I really appreciated the input.

Thanks to my illustrator Anna Hancock who designed Brad and Adam and their friends – I was so impressed when Brad and Adam were finally revealed. Thanks Anna.

To the cover designer, Emmantech Ltd, what a brilliant cover. Great work.

Last, but definitely not least, thank you GOD for trusting me to accomplish this.

Introduction

The reason for writing this book was to encourage and empower the everyday person to have a financial game plan for their finances. This is not a book to advise where to invest or what to invest in; nor is it a book on debt and the details involved in getting out of debt, though I do touch on these two topics in relation to planning your finances. This book is more about the utilisation of your money. It asks how do you utilise your money to get into debt or how do you utilise your money to become wealthy? Most people do not have a plan for their money; nor do they even think about such a plan. This book covers such an approach and explains how you can make your money work for you or against you.

I believe this book is a preventative book more than a cure, although it can be used both ways. I am a qualified accountant with many years' experience and have successfully managed a few finance departments along with giving finance and budgeting training to individuals. I have sat with many people who did not have such a plan and, because of this, found themselves drifting. I believe in all aspects of our lives we must have a plan, especially when it comes to our money. Most of us spend a whole day, five days a week, working hard to make money, but few of us ever think beyond this fact. We learn to live from pay cheque to pay cheque, drifting through life, and only realise too late that what we have been doing was not wise at all. In fact a lot of us have never been taught budgeting or how to plan. If this sounds familiar then this is the book for you, as it will definitely open your eyes to the possibilities money has to offer if you utilise it wisely.

Coming from an Asian Caribbean background I have seen both the prudent and the extravagant lifestyle while growing up. By the time I started working I had been both sensible and unwise with money. These experiences all helped form my thinking about money and taught me some valuable lessons. I learnt that being prudent will hold me in much better stead. After being unwise with my money and finding out I was in debt, I found I did not like that feeling and decided to take the principles I learnt in the past and apply it to my finances. It was difficult getting out of that debt, it took me about a year to get my finances in order. It was not a lot of debt but it was still twelve months out of my life in which I could have been making progress growing my finances and achieving my financial goals. I also felt quite embarrassed, as I am a qualified accountant and it is expected that I should know better when handling money.

We are all human and we all make mistakes. I do believe this book is going to help you in the way you handle money, and I hope that it will give you a new perspective for your own finances. If you have no financial goals at present, I hope this book inspires you to put some in place. It is unbelievable how having a goal to work towards can help us focus, and motivate us to achieve. This book is written to help you set this goal.

You may be in debt; this book is for you. You may not have any debt but are adrift with your finances; this book is for you. You may want to become wealthy and therefore need a game plan on utilising your money wisely; this book is for you. Finally you may be starting or thinking of starting your journey with making and spending money; this book is also for you.

This volume is the first installment in a series of books about my two fictional friends Brad and Adam and their colleagues Jennifer and Sally. The first few chapters are based on these four individuals and their financial approaches, explaining what was good about them and what was not. The remaining chapters then go into describing personal financial strategies: planning them, monitoring them, foolproofing them, and looking at how to avoid problems and events which may undermine them.

I am no advocator of debt but I do utilise it at times for my own purpose and to my benefit. Therefore, this book clarifies debt, both 'good' and 'bad', and looks at 'how to use it', 'when to use it', 'why to use it' and 'if you should use debt at all'.

For the purpose of this book I have assumed a monthly personal salary of £1,000 (or yearly personal salary of £12,000) **after tax and NI**, but the information and concepts can still be applied to the self-employed, temporary worker or contractor. By using a personal salary my aim was to make financial information and budgeting easy to understand and accessible for all reading this book. For the individuals who do not earn a yearly personal salary please tailor the information from this book to suit your individual need.

I must also mention the income and expenses in this book may not necessarily align with the income or expenses you will currently see in the so-called 'real world'. This is because monetary amounts can fluctuate constantly and from country to country. I have used the British '£' pound in the spreadsheets listed in this book but any currency symbol can be used. I have kept the figures simple and straightforward to comprehend, therefore this may not wholly reflect real income and real costs in everyday life.

I have arranged the book so you can refer to the glossary at the back when you come across a name or phrase you do not understand. Words in the glossary are in SMALL CAPS the first time they are mentioned in each chapter.

Now you know what is to follow, and because I know the benefits of a solid personal finance plan, I want to challenge you to develop one yourself. Let's get started!!!

I hope you enjoy this book and find it useful. For more information, please follow Brad and Adam on their website **www.bradandadamseries.com.**

Neala

1

THE HERE AND NOW

Brad has just completed university and is very excited about the future and his new job. He has recently been hired as a Computer Engineer with a reputable and well-established computer company called *Computer Express*. The company came to Brad's university and recruited four graduates from his Computer Science class. Working for *Computer Express* is a great opportunity as the company is expanding and growing rapidly. All four students are extremely pleased with their job offers and are looking forward to a rewarding career with this company. Brad is only 22 years old and feels he has hit the jackpot.

Brad really enjoyed his life at university and took out the maximum student loan possible. If Brad could have accessed more money – either as DEBT, a GRANT or a DISBURSEMENT from the university – he would have. Brad also has a bank account with a student OVERDRAFT FACILITY that he has fully tapped into. As a university student with no job he had maxed out all his avenues to borrow more money. Therefore, Brad is already starting his new career with a lot of debt. However, this is what he has seen growing up: his parents always lived for the now and enjoyed life; they tended not to deny themselves the things they wanted and Brad has learnt to be of the same mindset. He is really excited about getting all the latest stuff he has had his eye on, especially now as he has his degree and will be earning some decent money. Brad is optimistic as his starting salary is good and he expects his INCOME to grow as he progresses in his job. Therefore he decides to go on a spending spree and treat himself to a new car. After all the hard work and years at university it is time to reward himself; new car here we come!

It wasn't just a new car Brad ended up getting. He just couldn't help himself and ended up purchasing a new Swiss hand-made watch and some new suits for his workplace. After all, he must look the part. However, Brad still has two more months to go before he even starts his new job and three more months to go before he gets his first payslip. Therefore Brad now has more debt to his name and he hasn't even started his new job. Brad has already spent most of his first and second month's pay without even thinking about his new monthly costs now that he has left university. He will need to think about paying his rent and utility bills along with the additional cost of running a sports car, which can be very expensive to maintain. Where will the money come from for Brad to pay these bills?

2½ years after University

Brad and his stunning fiancée Eleanor are planning an extravagant wedding. One only gets married once in a lifetime, so it needs to be perfect. The wedding is beautiful and the bride's dress is magnificent. Everyone comments that it must have cost a fortune. The honeymoon is even better and the couple have a wonderful time on an exotic island. Brad had to take out another CREDIT CARD just to pay for this honeymoon as the wedding itself was so expensive, and they had already maxed out all their credit cards and additionally had to take out a LOAN to assist paying for the wedding. Actually a lot of Brad and Eleanor's friends are having the same type of wedding and luxurious honeymoon, so Brad and Eleanor are really just keeping up with the expectations of society, the expectations of their friends and the expectations of their families. Brad's parents insisted they have a beautiful wedding; it would be too embarrassing if everything was not up to the high standards of the weddings others were having. It is actually a new fad to have the dream wedding with the dream wedding dress and the dream honeymoon and unfortunately it is now common for people like Brad to pay for this via loans and credit cards.

Shortly after the honeymoon the couple decide to invest in a beautiful three bedroom house in one of the more expensive neighbourhoods in their area. Brad is young and has his whole life ahead of him. His mindset is to get these luxuries now and worry about how to pay for it later. This is the way he has been brought up, and it is all he knows. Like all of their friends, Brad and Eleanor also decided to take a holiday every year. They made this promise to themselves before getting married and intend on keeping up this goal regardless of what else happens in their lives. Both Brad and Eleanor are of the same opinion: spend now and pay for it later.

Brad also enjoys keeping up with all the latest products, especially the latest electronic gadgets. These gadgets tend to only have a short lifespan and therefore he must always replace them or be left behind. For Brad and Eleanor, appearances are important. Their thinking is "if all of our friends are living this lifestyle then why can't we?" Unfortunately, most people in our society also subscribe to this way of thinking.

5 years after University

Things have not been going so well financially for Brad and Eleanor. They now have two children and many bills to pay. Their monthly EXPENSES now far exceed their income and this is putting a huge strain on the marriage. Even though they cannot afford it, they decide to take out a new credit card to pay for a holiday. If you remember this was part of the goals they made when they got married. They hoped that this would help them bond as a family and let them forget about their problems, if only for a short time. Unfortunately, the economy has also changed and this is affecting Brad's company. Before, it was much easier for him to get a BONUS (extra money on top of his monthly pay) or a promotion with higher pay, but unfortunately the company has had to cut bonuses and promotions are a bit hard to come by these days. Brad is feeling despondent. It is not like he doesn't want to work harder and climb the corporate ladder, but the opportunities are either just not there or lots of other people are competing for the same opportunity or job.

10 years after University

The situation is now really bleak in Brad's family household. Brad and Eleanor are on the brink of BANKRUPTCY and divorce. The situation at home is tense and not a pleasant environment to live in. Brad is tired and looking much older than his age. He does not know what to do or who to turn to. He feels embarrassed and ashamed; his work is suffering because of his stress and the company *Computer Express* has stagnated. There is hardly any growth in the company. Employees are happy just to keep the jobs they've got as the country's economy has also stagnated and there are no new jobs on the job market.

Finances are so bad in Brad's family that he has fallen behind on his monthly MORTGAGE payments and the bank has come in and repossessed the family home. There was no way he could keep the house with the expensive mortgage payments and, because of all the debts he had accumulated over the years, he could not negotiate a deal with the bank. Brad is also behind on his credit card and loan payments along with other bills. The debts just keep accumulating and Brad is now ignoring all the bills that are coming in the post. He is really stressed and needs to visit the doctor. All the neighbours are whispering behind his back and Brad feels hopeless and humiliated; he feels he has let his family down and embarrassed them. Brad finally realises having debt is no joking matter.

Brad and his family have no choice now but to rent a house in a less desirable neighbourhood after losing their lovely family home. Brad has been severely depressed for a few months.

15 years after University

Brad and his family have massively downsized and continue to rent a smaller property. They drive one practical economical car and Brad now works an extra two weekends a month on top of his normal week to ensure all his expenses, including his debt payments, are paid. It was very difficult for Brad to find this weekend job as jobs are hard to find these days, but Brad is very willing and keen to get out of debt and knows he needs to pay the price to get out of this situation. Brad's wife Eleanor is also working longer hours to help subsidise the monthly income and assist in paying off the debt much quicker. It is a painful process but the family is all still together and also working together to assist in the situation.

This is very important. A support network can be a lifesaver when things are this bleak.

It is definitely not easy and a lot of the luxuries they would have had in the past are now gone, including the flashy sports car, which was sold at a car auction, and the hand-made Swiss watch was sold on an auction website.

Brad also visited a charity who sent him to a FINANCE COUNSELLOR. She really helped him to recognise where he went wrong and what he needed to do to sort things out. She assisted in giving him a FINANCIAL PLAN for getting out of debt and made sure he looked at all his bills, even the post (mail) that he had been ignoring for quite some time. Brad now realises what his exact financial position is – he can see this very clearly and knows it is not good. He is really grateful for this help and wished he had known about it earlier. Having this counsel has helped him to focus, which is greatly assisting him in coming out of his depression.

The one thing the family now have is peace of mind and each other, which is a massive help for Brad. He now has hope, and can see the time frame necessary to pay off his debt. It will take a lot of discipline, hard work and years, but he is committed and focused. I am sure we are all now rooting for Brad to succeed in getting out of debt.

Your choice

I do not want to give false hope; Brad's situation is bleak. It will take discipline and a lot of time for him to recover financially, but I must stress: the situation is not totally hopeless.

By the way, I would like to point out that Brad's story about how he got into debt is so much more than his personal behaviour towards money and spending. It is also **cultural**. This is very important to note. Yes, Brad was unwise with his money, I have been irresponsible with my money and I am sure many of you have been at some point. Remember we all live in a society geared towards debt, towards having things now and paying for them later. This is the western culture. Society seems to approve of people spending more than they EARN, taking out credit cards or loans and constantly being on trend in fashion and technology. These things can make it even more difficult for someone who has set his or her mind to be 'debt free' to get out of debt. Still it can be done; you just need to be more aware, clued up and determined.

My hope is that people will learn from Brad's situation and gain a better understanding of handling their finances wisely before they get into debt. Even though this is a fictional story it is very much based on real-life situations, including my own and from the many people I have counselled over the years.

For those of you reading this book, if you fall into Brad's situation, start addressing it before it escalates to his level. If it is at Brad's level then I have a few suggestions in the following pages. Bear in mind this book is not about **how to get out of debt** although there are a few helpful tips to follow.

Brad's story is a sad one and many people unfortunately fall into this trap. I hope this book inspires you to change your habits if you recognise you are in this situation.

CHAPTER SUMMARY

As we saw with Brad, spending habits can start from very early in life. It is worth studying your spending habits to see what they're like.

Ask yourself:

1. Do I buy items now and worry about how to pay for it later?

2. What are my family members' spending habits like?

3. Do I think my spending habits are manageable?

4. Do I ignore my post for fear of outstanding bills?

Having a FINANCIAL PLAN with clear goals can greatly assist a person in getting out of debt.

Having a support network of people can help in stressful situations.

The cultural or behavioural patterns of a society play a major role in forming our own personal habits. It is important we recognise this and develop a sensible custom. Following society's customs may not be good for us.

2

DEBT ANALYSIS
Stressed and Depressed

We have read the story of Brad's lifestyle along a ten- to fifteen-year time period. To the outsider looking at Brad and the way he lived in the first five years after university, it would seem that Brad was living the perfect dream: he had a beautiful house, the trendiest sports car and all the latest gadgets. Brad and his family also took a luxurious holiday every year, ate at the top restaurants and wore the latest fashion garments.

Who wouldn't want to have Brad's lifestyle? It looks like the perfect lifestyle. Unfortunately it is an illusion to the person looking in from the outside. On average, statistics confirm 30% or more of people living in western society live outside of their means, meaning they are spending more money than they earn. This is quite a large proportion of people when you really think about it. So many of us want to "keep up with the Joneses"– who are the Joneses and why do we feel the urge to follow in their footsteps? I have drawn a conclusion that there are no Joneses to keep up with. We are all trying to follow each other, not realising the nasty game of DEBT that a lot of us play. This book is a wake-up call; I want to say this loud and clear – **There are no Joneses; we do not need to keep up with them financially.**

I hope this brings some relief and freedom to you reading this. Debt is not a pleasant experience; actually it can be quite stressful and lonely. How did Brad get to this position? I am sure this was not what he planned for his life.

Let us look at where Brad went wrong:

> **Brad's expenses exceeds his monthly income**
>
> **Income < Expense = (Loss)**
>
> Your expenses exceed your income leaving you in a loss position at the end of the month.

Let's look at Brad's FINANCIAL STATEMENT. A financial statement in the context of this book takes into consideration both INCOME and EXPENSES over a period of time.

For ease of understanding, we will use a nice round salary figure for Brad of £1,000 per month of income after tax or an annual salary of £12,000 after tax. The principle is the same regardless of what salary you are earning monthly; either £500 or £5,000, in GB £, US$ or Euros €; the same principle applies.

Brad's monthly financial statement 1 month after University

DETAILS	£
Income	
Salary (after tax)	1,000.00
Total Income	**1,000.00**
Expenditure	
Rent	300.00
Car	200.00
Loans & Credit Cards	195.00
Utilities	180.00
Food	125.00
Fun & Entertainment	200.00
Total Expenditure	**1,200.00**
Loss	**(200.00)**

From this table we can see that Brad already has loans and credit cards he is paying off. He is also spending 20% of his income on 'Fun and Entertainment'. Brad is making an average monthly loss of £200. The brackets mean that Brad is in debt.

£1,000 – £1,200 = (£200)

From the table above we can see that on a monthly basis, Brad's expenses **exceed** his income by an average of £200.

19

Looking at this, it doesn't seem to be a big deal; he can put it on an OVERDRAFT or a CREDIT CARD and deal with it later. There does not seem to be a problem here. This is the illusion most of us have: we think we can handle having an average £200 a month DEFICIT; it appears to be easy to sort out over the next few months. To really understand this situation we need to take it further into the future.

Let's look at this breakdown after a year:

(£200) × 12 months = (£2,400) yearly loss

Now we can start seeing how Brad's expenses are growing compared to his income. When we look at the calculation above we can see that by the end of the year Brad has a £2,400 overdrawn amount. He could have played smart and kept this on an interest-free credit card or he could be paying interest on this amount. Either way he is in debt of £2,400 or more in just one year. To Brad and many other people, this does not seem too bad. Maybe it seems reasonable and something he feels he can pay off quite soon. In Brad's opinion this amount is quite manageable. This is where the trap starts to get laid. Instead of dealing with the problem now (because this is a problem) many people, including Brad, think they can handle the situation and put it off for the future. They think they can always rely on a BONUS or a promotion to pay this debt off, or they will win the lottery. It is easy to think of that imaginary income that comes magically from nowhere to pay off debt expenses. However, even if Brad was to get a bonus, because of his spending habit/patterns, it is more likely that he will spend this money on something else instead of putting it to good use and clearing his debts. This is a proven fact with many people: it is a lack of discipline where money is concerned that leads to and exacerbates financial problems, and far too many people think they are in control of their money rather than their money being in control of them.

Let's take this analysis even further:

5 years after University

We can see in the financial statement on the next page that Brad is really in a tricky situation now and where before he thought he could get on top of his debt, it now seems to be snowballing.

What do I mean by snowballing?

As an example let's look at an avalanche – how does it start? It starts as a tiny snowball that gains momentum as it continues rolling down the mountain, getting massively bigger and bigger and moving faster the closer it gets to the bottom. This is the same with debt. It starts off as non-existent. It gets to be a small problem, but as time goes on it can quickly develop into a massive problem.

This is what has happened to Brad's debt. It is called COMPOUNDING.

Brad's monthly financial statement 5 years after University

DETAILS	£
Income	
Salary (after tax)	1,000.00
Total Income	**1,000.00**
Expenditure	
Mortgage	550.00
Car	200.00
Loans & Credit cards	420.00
Utilities	190.00
Food	200.00
Fun & Entertainment	210.00
Total Expenditure	**1,770.00**
Profit / (Loss)	**(770.00)**

This table shows how Brad's expenses are growing significantly with time. If we take his monthly average loss and multiply it by 12 months it gives us a yearly loss position of £9,240. This is quite a huge amount and we have only looked at one year. What about the other four years?

COMPOUNDING

The debt accumulates interest in the first month. This makes the debt larger, and this happens every month thereafter until or unless the debt is paid off. Suddenly Brad is paying interest on top of his interest on his debt. Therefore what we are seeing is a rapid expansion of his interest payment on his debt.

As your debt grows so too do the interest payments. What makes it compound even quicker is that after a while, if you are not on top of your debt, then instead of getting low-interest payments, you now have higher rates because you have too much debt. The interest is now increasing your debt even faster than even you would have anticipated, leading to this avalanche. This is the shock for most people who often think they **have time.** Time to pay off their debts, only to realise with time the situation has grown way beyond them and they can no longer cope with the problem.

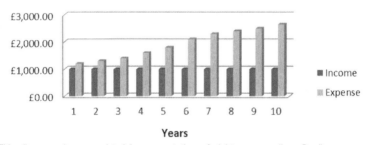

Brad's debt accumulation over a 10 year period before visiting the Financial Advisor

This diagram shows a pictorial representation of debt compounding. Brad's expenses significantly increase yearly compared to his income.

Brad is now on the verge of BANKRUPTCY and all aspects of his life are now affected. His marriage is affected, his children are affected and his quality of work is affected. Brad has too much on his mind and no solution to the problem. Debt affects the whole family; the home becomes a stressful environment to be in. Everyone is stressed, including the children. Not a pleasant environment to live in. I hope you understand the situation that Brad has in front of him.

What can Brad do?

Brad visits the FINANCE COUNSELLOR, and some of their recommendations are listed below. He will need to know his CREDIT HISTORY (CREDIT REPORT and CREDIT SCORE).

CREDIT HISTORY or CREDIT REPORT

A record of an individual's past borrowing and repaying, including late payments and bankruptcy.

CREDIT SCORE

This represents the creditworthiness of that person. Lenders use credit scores to determine who qualifies for a LOAN, at what INTEREST RATE, and what CREDIT LIMITS.

Brad can get this information from a credit scoring agency on a monthly or annual basis. For example, in Britain, Brad's credit score is a single number between 0 and 1000. If you live elsewhere, you will have to find out what score (if any) is relevant to your country; searching on the internet may be a good starting point. Depending on what this number is will depend on the rate of interest Brad will pay for borrowing. The higher your credit score, the better your credit rating. A high credit score means Brad will pay lower interest on any money he borrows or owes. A low credit score means he could end up paying huge amounts of interest on any money he borrows or owes. It is important that Brad protects his credit score; otherwise he will be wasting money paying unnecessary interest charges. This is where we previously spoke about the debt situation compounding or snowballing (a new debt multiplying the amount instead of simply adding to it). If Brad's credit score is poor then the interest he will be paying will be high. As of writing this book the companies listed in *Useful Information* are the most reputable and recognised in Britain for checking credit scores and can also assist you by giving advice in making your credit score better. I definitely advise speaking to them. I only recently did it myself as an annual check-up, sort of like a doctor's health check. I recommend having a financial check-up yearly as we can see the importance above of having this done. It can help save a lot of money when we borrow because if we have a good score we are able to borrow at cheaper rates. Your credit report will give you this full financial information.

I know there are quite a few people who think that checking their credit score will affect their credit rating. This is a myth. You can check your credit score as many times as you like and it will not affect your credit rating.

Secondly, Brad needs to cut up his credit cards. Especially if he knows he does not have control over them. He also needs to call any other organisation he owes money to and make arrangements to pay off his outstanding balance, letting them know what he can realistically afford and over what realistic time frame. In this situation Brad cannot afford to ignore these companies or their letters. If he explains his current situation and that he wants to get this sorted, they are more likely to be sympathetic towards him. Brad should not avoid any letters or phone calls concerning finances that come to his house. He should call them all and show his willingness to sort the problem out. This can sometimes be quite embarrassing, but it is better to face the embarrassment and get the matter sorted than leave it and let the situation get worse. I have known too many people who have ignored their letters and phone calls and the situation just got messier and messier until they ended up in court with a COURT JUDGEMENT and their name BLACKLISTED. A blacklisted name can take years to clear and is written very clearly on your credit report file for all banks and lending agencies to see.

A BLACKLISTED NAME
This means you may have defaulted on a debt or you are always very late in paying or unable to pay.

Thirdly, if Brad is finding it difficult handling his finances then a strategy he could adopt is the ENVELOPE SYSTEM. This is where Brad puts a set amount of money aside on a monthly basis for certain categories like food, shopping, eating out and other miscellaneous items. When the envelope money is gone then Brad has no more money left for that item category for the month. This system really helps people who are not disciplined or struggle to work with spreadsheets. I highly recommend it to those who struggle in this area, try it and see. I know we live in the age of online shopping, which can make the envelope system a bit hard for some people to implement and follow. Still, it has proven to be successful even in today's cashless age, although it does require a certain level of discipline and innovative thinking to succeed on your part. Please also refer to chapter 7, *Action Plan*, which talks about simple budgeting techniques, including setting up an income and expense spreadsheet and more useful tips

Fourthly, Brad and his wife Eleanor should have regular family meetings to discuss where they are financially and also to encourage themselves that they are making headway. For me this is extremely important, because right now this family needs some encouragement and motivation. They should also get the children (depending on their ages) involved in this discussion to some extent. The children need to realise the need for the family downsizing, and they need to be encouraged to play their part. This exercise is extremely important in maintaining family relations and also keeping communication channels open. Brad should not have to go through this whole process by himself; the encouragement of his family is vital.

Brad and Eleanor having regular meetings in a month to discuss their finances can help them keep on top of their monthly finance BUDGET. I know this helps because I encourage my clients to follow this same principle and they always know what they have to spend and save in any given month. This is especially useful more towards the end of the month when they know they have to watch their spending – making sure they do not overspend from this month taking that debt into the next month.

Brad should also seek out a person outside of the family that he can confide in. This can help greatly as it gives him an outlet where he can release his anxiety and stress. Ideally this person should have a really good track record with handling money or have been through a similar situation of debt and is now on a positive road to recovery to help them understand, support and motivate Brad. Brad needs hope right now and good counsel is often a massive help in times like these.

One of the ways Brad was able to cut costs was to pay off the debt with the highest interest first. This saved a lot of money in interest payments.

There are other measures the Finance Counsellor recommended: Brad gave up paid cable television and now has basic television channels, bought a cheaper car and uses public transport, cut down on eating out, he dropped his gym membership and now uses the park to exercise and the family sold quite a lot of their stuff, like unused gadgets, on auction websites to raise extra cash. All this extra money raised was used to clear their debts. Brad and his family also stay away from shopping centres as they just encourage them to spend.

The truth is Brad's situation is bad and it is going to take him a long time and a lot of effort to get out of this mess. We are looking at years of his life to rectify this. But it can be done.

Brad's monthly financial statement 10 years after University, and after visiting the Finance Counsellor

DETAILS	£
Income	
Salary (after tax)	1,000.00
Weekend job (extra hours)	250.00
Total Income	**1,250.00**
Expenditure	
Rent	300.00
Car	125.00
Loans & Credit cards	520.00
Utilities	150.00
Food	110.00
Fun & Entertainment	20.00
One-off expense fund	25.00
Total Expenditure	**1,250.00**
Profit / (Loss)	**0.00**

We can see Brad has implemented the recommendations of the Financial Advisor, especially when we compare this statement to the previous ones. Brad is now living a very frugal lifestyle with the majority of his income paying off outstanding debts.

For ease of understanding, we have only used Brad's salary and not included his wife Eleanor's.

Brad's monthly expenses 10 years after leaving University and visiting the Financial counsellor

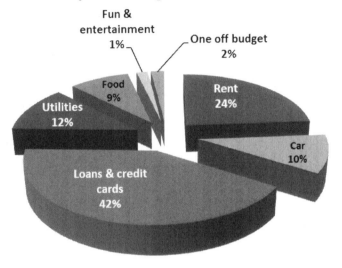

The pie chart shows that 42% of Brad's income now goes towards clearing his debts. This is a huge percentage (%) and Brad is living quite frugally on the remaining balance, as we can see from the diagram.

For me the answer to this problem is the preventative measure: try to avoid getting yourself into this debt situation, rather than having to cure being in debt and enduring the pain of getting out of it. I really wanted to paint the brutal picture of debt and what it can do to you, your family and your entire life.

I would also like to point out that I have excluded childcare costs from the expense section and partner's income (Eleanor's salary) from the income column in the spreadsheets listed. This is because I wanted to keep the income and costs simple, consistent throughout the book and, as I said previously, easy for all reading to understand. By no means does leaving this information out take away from the rationale portrayed in the spreadsheets.

Good debt vs. bad debt – the illusion

There have been lots of books and discussions about 'good debt' and 'bad debt'. I would tend to say debt is debt and it depends on the individual and the situation as to whether it is a problem or not.

Some debts are considered good; for example, obtaining a student loan to get a degree. But too often student loans are a starting point for getting into debt rather than a starting point for being good financial stewards.

Debt is debt, good or bad. A MORTGAGE can be a good debt or a bad debt, depending on the individual circumstances. If paying the mortgage on a monthly basis is eating into most of your income, leaving you to struggle to make ends meet, then it is definitely bad debt. A mortgage can be a good debt when, at the end of the month, you are able to meet all your monthly financial obligations without feeling stressed. It is so important that we do not fall into the trap of thinking about good debt verses bad debt; it all boils down to basic discipline and control. If you cannot handle the money you earn wisely, how can you handle the debt that is not yours wisely? That's just a thought I want to leave you with.

Refer to chapter 8 *Foolproof Your Game Plan* for a more in-depth discussion on 'Good debt vs. bad debt'.

CHAPTER SUMMARY

DEBT = INCOME < EXPENDITURE
Expenditure is greater than your income.

Drawing up a monthly BUDGET spreadsheet with INCOME AND EXPENDITURE can help you keep on top of your expenses.

Ask yourself:

1. What am I willing to give up that will save me money to clear my debts?
2. How many years is it going to take for me to clear my debt?

The definition of DEBT COMPOUND
When personal debt burden becomes so large it inevitably begins to fan ever higher interest payments leading to greater debt.

CHAPTER SUMMARY continued...

Having a good credit score and credit history can greatly assist you in saving money. *Do you know what yours is?*

Adopting the **ENVELOPE SYSTEM,** where you put aside money on a monthly basis for certain expenses, helps many people who are not disciplined or struggle to work with spreadsheets.

A BLACKLISTED NAME means you may have defaulted on a debt or you are always very late in paying or unable to pay.

MONTHLY EXPENSES are the monthly average of what you spend normally.

3

BREAKEVEN ANALYSIS
The Hidden Trap

BREAKEVEN ANALYSIS in the context of this book is:
Your **monthly** INCOME = your **monthly** EXPENSES
I emphasise the word monthly.

Jennifer was Brad's classmate at university, and was one of the four students recruited to work at *Computer Express*. She also earns the same salary of £1,000 per month after tax or £12,000 per year. Jennifer hates DEBT and, being quite a disciplined person and wanting to maintain her finances, she decided to go on a budgeting course at her local college to ensure her finances were always under control and that she is basically handling them correctly. Jennifer's story seems to be an admirable one. Let's dig deeper.

Jennifer's monthly financial statement 1 month after University

DETAILS	£
Income	
Salary (after tax)	1,000.00
Total Income	**1,000.00**
Expenditure	
Rent	275.00
Car	150.00
Loans & Credit cards	75.00
Utilities	200.00
Food	125.00
Fun & Entertainment	175.00
Total Expenditure	**1,000.00**
Profit / (Loss)	**0.00**

This budget looks to be fine with no problems. Jennifer is set to pay all her bills from her salary.

I have continued to use the £1,000 salary figure to keep the calculations simple. As we can clearly see from the diagram above, Jennifer's monthly income meets her monthly expenditures, bringing her to a zero balance at the end of the month. She has no remaining money at the end of the month. Looking at this analysis we can assume Jennifer is handling her finances wisely. Jennifer has ensured all of her **monthly** bills are taken care of. This is quite good for Jennifer to know this information and to balance it so evenly, where income exactly equals expenditure. Quite a large proportion of people in our society today do not even do this exercise.

1 year after University

Jennifer's monthly financial statement 1 year after University

DETAILS	£
Income	
Salary (after tax)	1,000.00
Total Income	**1,000.00**
Expenditure	
Rent	275.00
Car	150.00
Loans & Credit cards	75.00
Utilities	200.00
Food	125.00
Fun & Entertainment	175.00
Unexpected costs not budgeted	80.00
Total Expenditure	**1,080.00**
Profit / (Loss)	**(80.00)**

For the last few months, Jennifer has accumulated over £300 debt amount due to unexpected costs she had not foreseen and therefore had not budgeted for.

Jennifer suddenly realises her income has not met all her expenses for the year and is confused as to why. She thought she had budgeted correctly, what could have gone wrong?

This is where the problem arises with the breakeven analysis: Jennifer did not envisage and therefore did not BUDGET for her washing machine breaking down, meaning that she now needs to pay to fix her washing machine. On top of that, Jennifer needed to spend money on having an emergency dental procedure done to her mouth. These were sudden and unexpected bills. They are normal yearly expenses but most people tend to forget to budget for ONE-OFF EXPENSES. This is why I call it the **HIDDEN TRAP**.

Jennifer was under the impression she was on top of her finances. However, on closer inspection and looking at her monthly budget after a year instead of her first one month budget she gets a clearer picture and realises she is not.

Unfortunately this aspect of budgeting was not taught in the budgeting course she took a year ago.

Jennifer is actually on the road to debt accumulation. It may not be to the extent of Brad's situation, but debt does build up over time. Unfortunately, Jennifer needs to take out a CREDIT CARD to clear this balance, as there is no room in her monthly income to pay for these expenses. Jennifer now needs to come up with a new game plan in order to clear this credit card balance and really bring her finances in order.

5 years after University

Unfortunately Jennifer did not come up with a way to deal with this debt. She could have looked again at her monthly expenses to find ways of either cutting back or downsizing on an item in her expenses. If this were not possible she could even downsize small amounts from several items to build in these one-off expenses into her budget. Let's take this analysis further and see what has happened to Jennifer over a five-year period.

As we can see on the next page, Jennifer has not got on top of the one-off expenses. Looking at this analysis, she is really shaken up by what it shows. She thought she was handling her finances wisely, but this five-year analysis chart shows her that her debt has been growing. Not only that, but because she has left it for so long it is now starting to COMPOUND. If you remember from Brad's story, Jennifer will now also be paying higher INTEREST RATES, and the interest on top of interest will be leading to greater debt. As her debt has started to grow more quickly, Jennifer now feels that she is losing control of her finances. There is no room in her budgeting for any expenses other than her monthly ones, especially none for those one-off expenses that are a normal part of life. Jennifer therefore needs to take out a LOAN to pay these extra bills or put these expenses on an interest-free credit card and keep rolling the debt forward. But with this debt, will she even be able to get additional borrowing?

Jennifer's monthly financial statement 5 years after University

DETAILS	£
Income	
Salary (after tax)	1,000.00
Total Income	**1,000.00**
Expenditure	
Mortgage	400.00
Car	125.00
Loans & Credit cards	110.00
Utilities	170.00
Food	150.00
Fun & Entertainment	100.00
Unexpected costs not budgeted	95.00
Total Expenditure	**1,150.00**
Profit / (Loss)	**(150.00)**

As the table shows, Jennifer is incurring an average monthly loss of £150 or, multiplied by 12 months, an average yearly loss of £1,800. Most of this loss comes from the 'Unexpected costs not budgeted' section.

Let's take this analysis to ten years. I want to show you how debt creeps, crawls or suddenly appears all over you if you are not careful, even when you do think you are doing the right thing as many of you would assume you were doing by having your monthly income equal your monthly expenses.

Jennifer's monthly financial statement 10 years after University

DETAILS	£
Income	
Salary (after tax)	1,000.00
Total Income	**1,000.00**
Expenditure	
Mortgage	400.00
Car	125.00
Loans & Credit cards	200.00
Utilities	180.00
Food	150.00
Fun & Entertainment	75.00
Unexpected costs not budgeted	125.00
Total Expenditure	**1,255.00**
Profit / (Loss)	**(255.00)**

As described in the table Jennifer is incurring an average monthly loss of £255 or, when multiplied by 12 months, an average yearly loss of £3,060. More than half of this yearly loss is coming from the 'Unexpected costs not budgeted'. Jennifer's loans and credit card payments are also growing to assist in paying for this monthly average loss.

The situation now looks dire. It may not be as bad as Brad's, but it is definitely now out of control. Jennifer has become extremely stressed and has to seek out professional advice. In a way I feel really sorry for her as she thought she was handling her finances wisely, only to realise she is now in debt. She is also frustrated with herself for letting this get so out of control and wishes she had made the necessary changes four years ago instead of letting the debt grow.

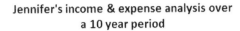

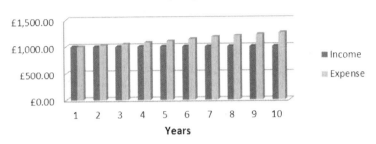

The diagram shows Jennifer's expenses increasing yearly compared to her income over a ten-year period.

For the readers living in Britain, please refer to the back of this book in *Useful Information* for advice and helpline numbers, which are useful if you find yourself in a similar situation. For my other readers the internet is a good starting point to gain information, or ask a professional person in this field for guidance. Even if the debt is small and you think you can manage it, it is sometimes wise to seek professional help and advice before it snowballs out of control.

It is time that we as individuals really start getting wise about our finances and try to avoid any unexpected problems that may allow us to enter into debt. In this situation, all Jennifer needed to do was build in a section to save for one-off expenses and let this fund build on a monthly basis. This is what I call a RAINY DAY FUND. It is for those hidden costs that are very much a part of our living expenses. Therefore this must be part of your monthly budgeting process, even if you don't use it that month and the fund keeps growing and growing. One day you will realise the need for it and be very grateful it was there.

10 year Analysis of Jennifer's expenses

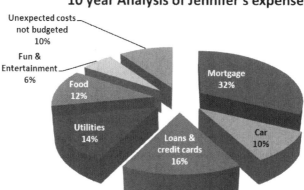

From the diagram, we can see that Jennifer is incurring 10% 'Unexpected costs not budgeted' out of her monthly average budget. These are costs Jennifer did not budget for and, if we refer to the previous table, caused her to incur losses. This increased her 'Loans & Credit card' cost, which are now 16% of her total expenses.

ONE-OFF EXPENSES FUND

(Otherwise known as a RAINY DAY FUND)

Can be defined as a fund for small, miscellaneous costs that arise in our day-to-day lives.

A rainy day fund can also be viewed as a short-term, easily-accessible, on-going fund. It must either be in an easy-access separate bank account or put aside in an envelope, and not locked away in a SAVINGS ACCOUNT that you cannot quickly get to when an emergency arises.

For the one-off expense fund I would recommend that you aim to put aside on a monthly basis an amount ranging from 4% to possibly 10% of your monthly salary after tax. This of course depends on your personal financial circumstances. As I said previously this one-off expense money may not even be spent in the given month **or** there may be a remaining balance at the end of the month. This money should therefore be carried forward to the next month, letting the fund grow until needed. I also use this system and know that most of the times there is no money to carry forward to the next month because there is always unexpected costs arising sometimes daily, weekly or monthly.

Every item we buy, be it a kettle, iron, mobile phone or a camera, has a useful economic lifespan and will eventually need to be replaced or fixed. Your rainy day fund covers such situations. It also covers things like gifts (birthdays, weddings, anniversaries) we may need to buy for friends and family, small emergency bills that occasionally arise and many other situations that crop up day-to-day. Having this fund and letting it build in the months we do not use it or start over when we do use it all is wise financial planning.

Monitor your one-off expense fund

If you do decide to put into action the one-off expense fund I would recommend monitoring it over a period of time. Ideally a three-month period. Undertaking this exercise can help to see if you have budgeted accurately for this fund. It could be you have not put in enough money and therefore have a shortfall (insufficient money to cover these expenses) in all three months. This is when you should either consider increasing the monthly amount of money you put into this category or re-analyse it to see if you are spending wisely. A three-month period should be a long enough time for examining this spending. If possible this fund should even itself out on a month by month basis.

It is a shame that the budget course Jennifer attended did not teach this. Jennifer really wanted to be sensible with her money but was not equipped with the right knowledge. She did plan her budget to the best of her understanding and even to get to that stage of knowing her monthly income and her monthly expenditure is good. Unfortunately, as you can see, it was not good enough. Hence the reason I have put in this chapter and called it the '**hidden trap**'.

To the person looking in from the outside, day-to-day all seemed fine, but the real truth is that Jennifer was living beyond her means. She needed to cut back on an expense, be it cable television or eating out, to make room for setting aside an amount on a monthly basis, and let this fund grow for when the occasion called to use it. If Jennifer had done this she may have been able to avoid getting into debt and thus avoided the stress she now finds herself with.

Key point

I must also stress, this does not necessarily mean we will always be on top of our finances by having this one-off expense fund, however it ensures that a good foundation is laid. There are many times other unforeseen circumstances can occur that throw us off guard, for example losing a job, an unexpected sickness, and so many other reasons that can cause one to accumulate debt. The one-off expense fund may or may not be able to help in such situations. But aside from these extreme situations, if you get the foundations of your budgeting right, there is little chance that debt should rear its ugly head in your life.

CHAPTER SUMMARY

A ONE-OFF EXPENSE FUND, otherwise known as a RAINY DAY FUND, can be defined as a fund for small, miscellaneous costs that arise in our day-to-day lives.

It is advisable to put aside an amount ranging from 4% to 8% of one's monthly income into a one-off expense fund and carry it forward into the following month if it was not fully used, thereby letting it grow until needed.

Monitoring this fund over a three-month period is wise. It could be that you need to increase or decrease the amount needed in this fund. A three-month period gives you that time of examination.

Every item we have or buy has a useful economic life span and will eventually need to be replaced or fixed.

We must remember to budget for gifts, entertainment, a friend or family in need etc. The one-off expense fund covers these sorts of things.

SAVINGS ANALYSIS
Peace of Mind

We will look at a good friend of Jennifer's; her name is Sally. As you can gather from the theme of the book Sally also went to the same university, graduated the same time and got hired at *Computer Express* along with Brad and Jennifer. For simplicity's sake, Sally also works for the same salary of £1,000 after tax per month or £12,000 after tax per year.

Both Sally and Jennifer took the same budgeting course at their local college when they started working at *Computer Express*. However, Sally decided to ensure her BUDGET had

room for ONE-OFF or RAINY DAY EXPENSES as she realised early on in her career, after a few hard knocks to her EXPENSES, that this was crucial. Since Sally had learnt this lesson early on and found it stressful, she decided to have two types of funds in her monthly expense column: the ONE-OFF EXPENSE FUND and the SAVINGS FUND. For Sally they are totally different funds with different uses.

Why has Sally decided on this course of action?

Sally has set a goal for her finances, which involves a long-term plan of five to fifteen years. She wants to save up for a DEPOSIT for a house in her first five years after university and have her MORTGAGE completely paid off for her house in the following ten years, if finances continue as she plans, or hopefully no longer than fifteen years if other unexpected situations arise. This is quite an ambitious goal, but with discipline and proper goal setting in her budget, Sally should not have any difficulties accomplishing this. It may mean a bit of sacrifice in other areas of spending but I think Sally is in the right frame of mind to accomplish this. Let's now take a look at the details:

Sally's monthly financial statement 1 month after University

DETAILS	£
Income	
Salary (after tax)	1,000.00
Total Income	**1,000.00**
Expenditure	
Rent	260.00
Savings fund	100.00
Car	110.00
Loans & Credit cards	50.00
Utilities	140.00
Food	135.00
Fun & Entertainment	135.00
One-off expense fund	70.00
Total Expenditure	**1,000.00**
Profit / (Loss)	**0.00**

We can see both the 'Savings fund' and the 'One-off expense fund'. Sally's budget is a sensible and stable budget. Sally also had a small student loan that she is paying off in the section 'loans & credit cards'

All looks fine with this table; we can see clearly the one-off expense fund and the savings fund. From looking at this table, we also see that Sally has decided not to spend extravagantly on FUN & ENTERTAINMENT and to keep her car fund to a minimal. Sally's goal is to put at least 10% of her monthly INCOME into her savings fund.

Sally's monthly financial statement 1 year after University

DETAILS	£
Income	
Salary (after tax)	1,000.00
Total Income	**1,000.00**
Expenditure	
Rent	260.00
Savings fund	100.00
Car	110.00
Loans & Credit cards	50.00
Utilities	140.00
Food	135.00
Fun & Entertainment	135.00
One-off expense fund	70.00
Total Expenditure	**1,000.00**
Profit / (Loss)	**0.00**

The table shows no unforeseen circumstances and shows Sally is on track with her budget. Sally is getting her budgeting right.

For the year, Sally had to use some of her one-off expense fund for unexpected costs like fixing her refrigerator, which suddenly stopped working. Since the one-off expense fund existed, she was able not to touch her savings, which she has big plans for (putting down a deposit for a house in the next four years). Sally seems to be on the right track.

Sally's monthly financial statement 5 years after University

DETAILS	£
Income	
Salary (after tax)	1,000.00
Total Income	**1,000.00**
Expenditure	
Mortgage	400.00
Savings fund	100.00
Car	110.00
Loans & Credit cards	0.00
Utilities	140.00
Food	120.00
Fun & Entertainment	60.00
One-off expense fund	70.00
Total Expenditure	**1,000.00**
Profit / (Loss)	**0.00**

Sally has bought her house, as seen by the mortgage column, and has also paid off her student loan. She now has no loans or credit cards. The table shows no unforeseen circumstances. Sally is on track with her budget.

Sally's finances are really looking good. Her one-off expense fund basically evens itself out yearly, therefore taking care of any of those unexpected circumstances that arise in our daily life. It also means she does not need to touch her savings.

Hooray! Sally has bought her house as planned at the end of her five year period and was able to put down a good deposit. She is extremely pleased and realises that having this goal in place has really helped her to focus. The focus and sacrifice in her spending and saving habits have so far paid off.

I must mention that Sally's house deposit and her mortgage for the purpose of this book are in line with her salary and may not necessarily align with the house prices or mortgages you will see currently in the property market. This was done for the reason of keeping figures easy and simple to understand and therefore will not agree with what you know an average house or mortgage cost should be. As I have stated previously, this also applies to all the costing used in this book.

Sally is now focused on her ten- to fifteen-year goal of having the mortgage for the house completely paid off. She is excited by the actual purchase of the house. Accomplishing this has motivated her to continue with the next leg of her journey of paying off her mortgage. Sally is feeling good about life and, even though she has had to do without certain luxuries in order to accomplish her goal, she believes it is worth it.

Sally has been speaking with Jennifer, who was explaining the difficulties she has been having with her finances. Jennifer told Sally that this all arose from not having a one-off expense fund and now she has found herself in DEBT. Sally sympathises with Jennifer but is also glad she made plans early on to prevent herself from getting into debt, and that she put the rainy day fund into place. Except for her mortgage, which Sally sees as good debt, she is totally debt free. She has peace of mind, something Brad and Jennifer are lacking but wish they had.

Sally's monthly financial statement 10 years after University

DETAILS	£
Income	
Salary (after tax)	1,000.00
Total Income	**1,000.00**
Expenditure	
Mortgage	400.00
Savings fund	100.00
Car	110.00
Loans & Credit cards	0.00
Utilities	140.00
Food	120.00
Fun & Entertainment	60.00
One-off expense fund	70.00
Total Expenditure	**1,000.00**
Profit / (Loss)	**0.00**

Sally's income & expense statement shows no shocks; Sally seems to have got her budgeting right. She is financially prepared for any unforeseen circumstance.

Sally is going around the office with her good news; she's paid off a large chunk of her mortgage. All her hard work and discipline is being rewarded. Sally knows she needs to continue to be focused, but the end goal of the 'House being debt free' is pushing her on. Unfortunately Sally's car suddenly breaks down and will be too expensive to fix. Sally does not have enough money in her one-off expense fund to afford fixing the car. It is on its last legs so Sally decides to buy a new one.

She sits down and does her CAR COST calculations and realises she needs to tap into her savings account, as this is a big cost item. Sally does not want any other debt other than her mortgage, so she pays for the car outright with money taken from her savings and does not take out a LOAN as most people normally do. This situation sets Sally back and she finds it really hard; it can sometimes hurt when the goal boundaries are pushed back making the process longer. She feels a little bit flustered but finds it within herself to re-focus, and regroups. Sally has to keep her eyes on the end goal of 'Paying off her mortgage'. Having these financial goals in place are really helping her to focus.

Sally's monthly financial statement 17 years after University

DETAILS	£
Income	
Salary (after tax)	1,000.00
Total income	**1,000.00**
Expenditure	
Mortgage	0.00
Savings fund	100.00
Car	75.00
Utilities	140.00
Food	150.00
Fun & Entertainment	150.00
One-off expense fund	70.00
Total expenditure	**685.00**
Profit	**315.00**

Sensible and stable budgeting has paid off, and is still paying off for Sally. The mortgage section is now zero: '0'. Sally has a lot more money suddenly available to her, as can be seen with the profit figure of £315. In addition, Sally is still saving.

Sally has finally paid off her mortgage. It took her a total of seventeen years; from saving for the deposit, which took five years, to owning the house and paying it off for twelve years. What a relief this is for Sally! It took her two years longer than she anticipated due to the unexpected purchase of the new car and having to tap into her savings fund to pay for it. All those years of saving and sacrifice has finally paid off. Sally celebrates with her family. This is a great accomplishment; few people pay off their mortgage sooner than the mortgage end date but Sally has done it; good for her!

I would like to add that on average it normally takes a person twenty to thirty years **from date of purchase** to pay off their mortgage. Some people take even longer, and some never achieve this goal because they keep RE-MORTGAGING their property. This means taking out more debt on the house than the original mortgage. Some people re-mortgage to buy bigger houses or pay off existing debts, or even to have more spending money for things like holidays. Sally has done exceptionally well to have achieved this goal. I believe that she was able to do this because she had set a goal for her savings.

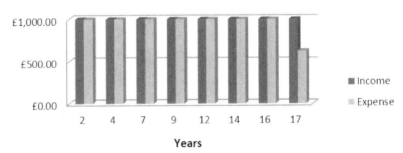

Sensible and stable budgeting has paid off for Sally. As we can see in the diagram, in year 17 she suddenly has a larger income than expenses. We see this in the sudden drop in the chart.

Sally now has more money available to her on a monthly basis; her mortgage payment can now be extra money to add to her savings. Let's look at the diagram for a better understanding.

Sally's monthly expenses 17 years after leaving University

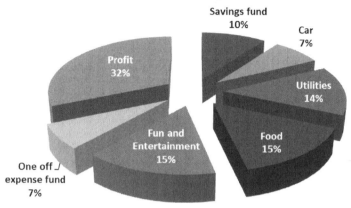

We can see that Sally no longer has a mortgage or any other debt. Sally now has more money than she has budgeted for, as we see in the pie chart, which shows a 32% profit,

Sally can now enjoy life more after years of denying herself and cutting back on certain luxuries that others were having. A few months after paying off her mortgage, she treats herself and her family to a two week luxurious holiday abroad. She can afford to do this because she has more cash available to her. Before paying off her mortgage, Sally and her family could afford no more than a week away with a few short weekend breaks on a yearly basis. Well now she can enjoy the finer things that she previously denied herself, and having this extra mortgage money is such an added bonus.

I do think Sally deserves to treat herself. As Sally has developed the habit of saving, and it is now part of her monthly routine, Sally has continued to save 10% or more of her monthly income even after paying off her mortgage. With these savings Sally and her family have set certain goals, like having more up-market family holidays compared to the ones they had before. Sally realises good planning and diligence really does pay off, even when it appears that others around you are enjoying life with good cars and holidays while you sacrifice. Sally sees this, especially after talking with Jennifer and seeing how stressed she has become over the years. Sally feels really sorry for Jennifer and decides to help her with her budgeting. Sally is so grateful she did not get into the debt trap especially seeing that Jennifer has had to downsize to even meet her monthly payments. Jennifer looks at her friend and is very happy for her, but still can't help that feeling of envy. Jennifer's favourite words now are 'if only': 'If only I had a rainy day fund.'; 'If only I had not let the situation get out of hand.'; 'If only I had paid the price at the time.'

Definition of a savings fund and how it is different to the one-off expenses fund

As we saw in Jennifer's story, the one-off expense fund can be defined as a fund for small, miscellaneous costs that arise in our day-to-day lives. It is sometimes viewed as a short-term, easily-available and accessible on-going fund.

> **SAVINGS FUND**
>
> A longer-term outlook and for longer-term goals. The goal can be specific or general. A lot of people like to put aside money monthly in a savings fund for the simple purpose of having peace of mind.

Therefore a savings fund is good for two reasons: it helps a person develop the habit of putting aside money, which is very hard in today's lifestyle and society; and, as I said before, it gives the individual peace of mind that is worth its weight in gold, especially in today's stressful and fast-paced environment.

It differs from a one-off expense fund in that firstly, the money can be locked away in a savings account, which comes with a bonus of having higher interest rates on your savings than if the money was kept in a regular bank account, known as a current account in Britain; and secondly, the use for the money is planned for, unlike the one-off expense fund that exists for situations requiring money to be used immediately.

I do know there are a lot of people who do not plan for their savings, but wouldn't it be greater for them if they did? I want to say that savings can be used for unexpected situations, like if a person suddenly loses their job. They can even be there for use with the possibly unforeseen news that you are expecting a baby. Having a savings fund can relieve a lot of stress with such unexpected information. These are extreme examples but they can happen in life, and these will be the times to tap into your savings.

Most of the time people aim to have three to six months of their monthly expenses saved. I would personally recommend this, simply for the peace of mind it brings to you. You can also put aside savings for other uses, for example taking a holiday, buying a car, saving for a deposit for a house, paying off an existing mortgage, for a wedding or honeymoon, financing a professional course or for occasionally treating yourself to some sort of luxury. It really depends on the person as to what the money can be used for. This is why I have called this book 'What is YOUR Financial Game Plan?' This is personal to you. All I can do is get you thinking about your money and the reasons why you might want to **start** saving or for what purpose you are **currently** saving. Even if you do not have a purpose for saving or can't think of one it is still a good habit to get into, putting aside money each month.

Saving funds can be broken down into different categories, some shorter term than others. You can put your savings into different savings accounts, even with different banks depending on your uses and access needs. Some savings can be locked away with the bank for long periods like five to ten years, which would mean higher interest rates the longer you lock it away for. Alternatively some savings can be locked away for shorter time frames like three months to a year but they are not likely to get as good an interest rate as if it was locked away for a longer period.

Remember there are no hard or fast rules to saving. These are just guidelines that can give you direction and purpose, depending on the goals you personally set.

Defining savings

> **Savings**
>
> Putting money into virtually RISK-free FINANCIAL VEHICLES or instruments where it can grow slowly and safely over time.

It is important to understand that saving is not risk taking and brings in little or no return. This money should be put into an interest-bearing account or into a unit trust cash fund. This money is not for INVESTING but for safe return over time.

I know for some of you reading this chapter you may feel that saving 10% of your monthly income is a daunting task, especially if you are someone who has never saved before. This is one of the reasons I have written this book, to help those of you who have never saved, or thought of saving before. Hopefully now you are thinking of saving, and your individual **reasons** are emerging in your mind.

Starting to save when you have never done so before can be challenging. I know this because I have counselled many people in this situation. A piece of advice I give to my clients: **If you as an individual set your mind to SAVE you can SAVE no matter how big or small an amount.**

I also know that for some people, starting to save can be more difficult, especially for university students with debt or young people starting off living on their own and paying their own way. I would recommend getting pen and paper out now while this chapter is fresh in your mind and jotting down your income and expenditure. *You can use the blank income and expenditure sheet included in the* Action Plan *chapter to do this exercise.*

After you have done this task (which may have been simple for some people and for others extremely difficult) and now you know your monthly income and expenditure, take some time to think your spreadsheet through. I would recommend taking a week to really analyse this from beginning to end. Be brutally honest. Ask yourself: 'Am I really spending my money wisely?' and 'Are there any areas I can cut back on?'

After you are satisfied that your figures and amounts are as accurate as you can get them, and you have highlighted where (if any) you can cut back on, then decide what you can realistically afford to save monthly. Even if you do not currently have a goal in mind for your savings, at least start the process of actually saving.

There are some people who, after looking at their income and expenditure, realise they can save 10%. If you can save 10%, that is great!

£1,000 (salary) × 10% (savings %) = £100

Some people can save more than 10%. If you can honestly save more than 10%, then that is even better, but I would first of all recommend reading the *Wealth Analysis* chapter on how to effectively utilise all your savings money, depending of course on your financial game plan.

There are then the people who would not be able to save 10% but they can definitely save something monthly. Start small; if it is 2% of your monthly income or 9% of your monthly income that goes into savings this is still great news.

£1,000 (salary) × 2% (savings %) = £20

£1,000 (salary) × 9% (savings %) = £90

Developing the habit of saving is sometimes better than the savings amount itself.

Unfortunately, some people cannot save because their expenditure is greater than their income. I would recommend paying off your debts before starting to save. Refer to Brad's story in the debt chapters for help and guidance.

Which savings group above do you fall into?

Fixed savings vs. percentage savings

I would like to draw your attention to two strategies you can use for saving:

1. Saving a **fixed** monetary amount on a monthly basis, for example saving £100 every month

   or

2. Saving a **percentage** (%) of your monthly salary like the example used in this chapter where Sally saves 10% of her monthly income.

Most of us would be familiar with the FIXED RULE APPROACH, as it is commonly used and quite straightforward to start, easy to set up with our banks and simple to maintain. This way, the same amount is saved every month or every year regardless of any increase or decrease in your income. It is a simple and easy policy.

Some of us may recognise the PERCENTAGE RULE APPROACH, which can be technical and not as easy to maintain. But the benefit of using this approach is that when your salary increases or you get additional income like a BONUS or monetary gift, you can easily apply the percentage rule and save money from these sources also. Similarly if your income decreases the saving percentage rule takes this into consideration. Comparatively, if it is a fixed amount you save monthly then it does not matter when additional income comes in or what that amount is. Therefore the fixed rule approach is inflexible to increases or decreases in income, whereas a percentage amount is adaptable to these situations. With the percentage rule it is much easier to work out what to save when the income increases, the amount of savings increases even if the percentage itself stays the same. This is especially useful for contractors, temporary workers or the self-employed whose income may not be stable on a monthly basis.

Let's look at an example:

	Income	Fixed amount per month	Percentage amount (10%)
June	£1,000	£100	£100
July	£900	£100	£90
August	£1,200	£100	£120
September	£1,250	£100	£125
October	£1,000	£100	£100
November	£1,350	£100	£135
December	£1,000	£100	£100
Total savings		**£700**	**£770**

Using the fixed rule is easy to apply and we can set a guaranteed monthly deduction of £100 with our bank

The percentage rule is not as easy to apply, especially when our income fluctuates, but it guarantees our savings increase with our income, be it from bonuses, promotion or monetary gifts.

Sometimes the increase can be quite significant, as we can see in the diagram. The fixed amount came in at £700 but the percentage amount came in at a staggering £770.

Therefore I would personally recommend using the percentage rule, especially if you have fluctuations in income. That way you can account for any income, no matter how small, to give an increase in savings. If it is likely to be more hassle to implement then use the fixed rule, or get someone to help you implement the percentage rule into your costing. Either is better than none.

Let's first say you **must** save. Saving should be a habit we all build into our lives. I would say start with being realistic: ask yourself, **'in my present situation how much can I realistically save?'** If you have never saved before and have never had self-control with your finances, I would recommend starting off small using 2% of your monthly salary.

Don't forget this money must be put in a safe place like a bank savings account or unit trusts. Sometimes it is good to put it where it is difficult for you to access this money immediately, especially if you have low self-control where spending is concerned. Alternatively, it might be more beneficial for you to put your money into an instant-access or short-term savings account, if you have a more immediate goal for this money and feel you can remain in control of it. Only you can know which of these is best for you, so please put the proper measures in place to safeguard this money and only use it for what it is intended for. You alone will know what your financial strategy is after fully reading this book.

Whoopee! We are on our way to a positive financial game plan.

CHAPTER SUMMARY

SAVINGS is putting money into virtually RISK-free FINANCIAL VEHICLES so it can grow slowly and safely over time. Developing the habit of saving is sometimes better than the savings itself.

SAVINGS FUND – normally aim to have three to six months EXPENSES saved in the fund, and most of the time this exists for a long-term outlook or for long-term goals. The goal can be specific, or to simply have peace of mind.

There should be a purpose for saving although any saving is better than no saving.

It is good to use either one of these strategies for saving:

1. FIXED RULE APPROACH

Saving a fixed monetary amount of your monthly income.

2. PERCENTAGE RULE APPROACH

Saving a percentage (%) of your monthly income.

If you have low self-control concerning spending then it is wise to put your savings where it is difficult for you to access immediately. Lock the savings away!!!

5

FRUGAL LIVING

This is the chapter of the book most people want to read and sometimes they skip the rest of the chapters just to get to this section. If you have done this I would recommend starting at the beginning of the book and reading all the chapters. There is useful information in the previous chapters that can help you.

As you are already aware, Brad, Jennifer and Sally all went to the same university, attended the same course and were recruited by *Computer Express* as part of their new recruits programme. We have all read their individual stories. Adam (a friend of Brad, Jennifer and Sally), also shared this same experiences as the others. However, he did things differently again. We now come to what I personally think is the best story: *The Wealth Creation Story*.

What we must first understand about Adam is that he is extremely ambitious and focused, and has a goal to become wealthy. Yes, Adam wants to acquire wealth, and working at *Computer Express* is a stepping stone for Adam achieving this.

Let's look at Adam's story.

From very early on in his life Adam has been disciplined in his finances. He would save roughly 10% or more of whatever INCOME he received. As a child he started this habit by saving a part of his monthly allowance from his parents. Since Adam was so disciplined in his finances, and because he knew he did not want to be in DEBT, Adam was able to pay part of his university tuition fees from these SAVINGS. During his time at university, he worked as a waiter and used his earnings to pay off the remaining part of his university fees. So he is starting his new job debt free. It took a bit of sacrifice and hard work but Adam is quite pleased with this accomplishment.

Adam has a FINANCIAL PLAN to become wealthy. He will save at least 10% of his income for savings and at least another 10% of his income for INVESTMENT. At the moment, he does not know what to invest in but he is sure an OPPORTUNITY will arise some day and wants to be prepared with a readily available CASH FLOW if and when one occurs.

3 years after University

Adam is living in a one bedroom flat with his wife Sue. They drive his small car from his university days. Things are a bit tough for Adam, especially when he looks at his work colleagues Brad and Jennifer earning the same income but appearing to live the good life. Sometimes he feels discouraged and down, and wonders if his plan of becoming rich will ever succeed. In the last three years, Adam has invested in a few projects, one of them being a small motorcycle shop that a friend decided to open. At the time, he thought the idea to be brilliant and got really excited but the business went bust and Adam lost all his investment money. After this, he went through a period of feeling despondent and considered giving up on his dream of being wealthy. However, Adam knows that hard work, determination and focus pay off, and he is soon back to his normal ambitious self. The one thing he learnt through the failure of the motorcycle business, which will prove to be invaluable in the future, is what to look for in order to run a successful business. He realises in order to get anywhere in life you have to take risks, but it is important to make sure they are calculated. This means doing thorough homework beforehand on any investments and it should prove to be profitable.

This bad business investment hurt Adam very deeply because he had worked very hard to save that money and he is sacrificing certain privileges to attain his goal. The next time he goes into a business venture he promises himself not to make the same mistake. He will do his homework and research the investment thoroughly before putting his money into it.

5 years after University

Adam has been involved in several business start-ups and has already made decent returns from his investments. He is slowly seeing his dreams become reality. It is not at the pace he anticipated but Adam is earning his salary and on top of that now has an additional income from other businesses. To celebrate, he decides to treat himself and his wife to a new car. Adam also reinvests the additional income he is receiving back into his investments. He is still very much focused on attaining his goal of being wealthy.

Adam is also very grateful to his wife who has the same goal and has also sacrificed along the way in order for them to achieve this. He realises that if his wife was not in agreement with him there would be no way he could have been able to accomplish this goal of becoming wealthy. Before Adam married Sue, he had sat down with her and told her about his dreams and aspirations, and he also told her about the sacrifices it would entail. Sue came into the relationship well prepared, and this is what has given them continued peace of mind and focus when around them friends and work colleagues all seemed to be living the good life while Adam and Sue seemed to be struggling.

10 years after University

Adam and Sue are now in a much different situation. All the hard work, diligence and sacrifice have paid off. Adam is now running two very successful businesses and has money invested in other areas that are returning a profit and income. His monthly investment income now exceeds his monthly salary income from his work place. He still currently works for *Computer Express*; however, he will be leaving his job later this year. Adam and his wife have now bought a lovely house in a very good neighbourhood. Their monthly mortgage payment is quite small because they were able to put down a large DEPOSIT on the house, also meaning they were able to get quite a good INTEREST RATE on the MORTGAGE. Adam sees this debt as good debt, especially with the low interest rate.

Adam is very glad he stuck with this strategy as he now sees Brad's and Jennifer's situations and how they are finding it hard coping with debt. Brad has aged quite considerably and Jennifer looks extremely stressed. Brad is also quite envious of Adam's accomplishments, especially as Brad use to laugh at Adam's tough lifestyle back in the early days while Brad was living it up. How the situations have turned around! Adam is quite glad he was able to stick to his game plan and not let other people's opinions sway him from accomplishing his goal. Adam feels sorry for Brad but realises Brad has made his own bed by the choices he decided to make with his money.

15 years after University

Adam has long left his job at *Computer Express* and now spends his time between his investment projects. He has no debt and his savings and investments just keep growing; in fact they are multiplying every year. Adam and his wife Sue are now able to travel and enjoy the fruits of their labour. Even though they are now living the good life, Adam maintains the discipline he has developed and is still extremely careful with his finances.

The one thing you learn on the way to WEALTH acquisition is that it is accomplished through a certain level of success. The knowledge used to gain this eventually becomes second nature, and it is then easier to grow your fortune than it was in the early days. Much like Adam found, although this was not easy or cheap for him. We can see here that COMPOUNDING is possible for gaining wealth, as well as accruing debt.

Adam's story is very admirable, but it came at a huge price in the early years. It also came with a lot of discipline and restraint, especially when he looked at other people's lives and saw how they were living. Adam could have been tempted into enjoying life in the now, like Brad. Thank goodness he was not and his diligence and determination has now paid off. With Adam's story we realise dreams can come true.

Key point

No matter what your age, you can be in your early twenties or late fifties, keep in mind that you are never too early or too late to come into the investing arena. It all depends on the financial goals you set out for yourself to achieve, your time frames for achieving them and your persistence toward gaining success in attaining them. My husband and I started our investment strategy in our early thirties and not straight out of university like Adam did. We wished we had known about this investment-saving tactic from very early on, as Adam did, but this was not the case. Nevertheless it has definitely not put us off from saving to invest, actually investing, and from wanting to achieve success in our investments. I hope this does the same for you.

CHAPTER SUMMARY

To create WEALTH one must have at least two of these qualities; ambition, focus, discipline, determination, persistence or a hard-working ethos.

Forming good habits with money both in spending and SAVING will assist in wealth creation.

Ask yourself:

1. What FINANCIAL GAME PLAN am I willing to implement to gain wealth?
2. Do I have the qualities (ambition, focus, hard-working etc.) that will be necessary in making wealth?

If a project you have invested in fails, do not worry as it can teach you an important lesson and help you know what not to do in the future. Learn from these set-backs, and other people's failures and mistakes as Adam learnt from Brad and Jennifer.

Having your family's support and agreement is vital on your journey to creating wealth, especially in times of set-back and discouragement. *Are your family in agreement with you?*

Thorough homework done on each INVESTMENT beforehand should prove to be profitable and also avoid failure.

Knowledge in your area of business will help your wealth grow. This can take time and effort to acquire and is not an overnight process. *Are you willing to pay the price to gain this knowledge?*

6

WEALTH ANALYSIS
Relieved and Happy

Before we get into this chapter it is important that we define INVESTING.

INVESTING

Putting money into financial or non-financial vehicles and instruments that have some degree of RISK in the hope of seeing the money grow significantly over time.

NON-FINANCIAL VEHICLES can include running your own small business or going into partnership with another business, it can be investing in an already existing business or it can be investing in property, either commercial or residential.

FINANCIAL VEHICLES can include investing in the stock market e.g. via shares, bonds, ETF's (Exchange Traded Funds) or unit trusts.

Let's now delve into the chapter and see what Adam does.

I am sure we were all inspired by reading Adam's story, but I am also sure many of us think that the sacrifice and effort needed to accomplish this is a lot. The truth is it does take a lot of effort and sacrifice to acquire WEALTH, especially if you do not come from a wealthy background or are not left a fortune in someone's 'will'. To make and grow wealth will require discipline, dedication, sacrifice and effort. I know a lot of people think they will continue to play the lottery and this will bring wealth, but I know a lot of older people who have given the lottery company so much money over the years and still never won anything. They are still to this day waiting for this illusionary wealth to come in. True wealth needs to be built. All wealthy people started from somewhere, and yes, there may be times when becoming wealthy come quite easily to some people. However, these numbers are few and far between. For the average Joe Blogs, meaning you and me, making wealth will be a process built on discipline and hard work. Statistics show that 10% or less of people hold wealth or what we perceive as being wealth. This means that 90% of people do not hold wealth. This should tell you how difficult it is to make wealth or to even keep it. Therefore, if you do not have a FINANCIAL PLAN with goals mapped out and a clear strategy then how are you to make wealth?

Let's see the strategy Adam used and break it down so that we can all understand how his plan was achieved:

We can clearly see from the table over the page that Adam has a 10% goal for SAVINGS and a 10% goal for investment. He and Sue then live off the remaining 80% of their combined salary, which also includes a RAINY DAY FUND. Adam went to a wealth creation seminar upon leaving university, hence the reason for his BUDGET being set out this way. We can also clearly see from the table that 80% of his salary is not a lot and he is intent on having no DEBT. During these early days, Adam and Sue were living quite frugally. This reminds me of a passage I read in Warren Buffet's biography that explains how Buffet did not spend money unless he had to in the early part of his wealth accumulation; actually Buffet lived quite frugally in his early days of making wealth. By the way Warren Buffet is one of the wealthiest men in the world. You should try to read his early story; it is inspiring.

WHAT'S YOUR FINANCIAL GAME PLAN?

Adam's monthly financial statement 1 month after University

DETAILS	£
Income	
Salary (after tax)	1,000.00
Total Income	**1,000.00**
Expenditure	
Rent	275.00
Savings fund 10%	100.00
Investment fund 10%	100.00
Car	90.00
Loans & Credit cards	0.00
Utilities	150.00
Food	125.00
Fun & Entertainment	90.00
One-off expense fund	70.00
Total Expenditure	**1,000.00**
Profit / (Loss)	**0.00**

A frugal budget that includes an 'Investment fund', a 'Savings fund' and a 'One-off expense fund'. Adam is living a very prudent lifestyle. Where is this budget taking him?

82

Adam's monthly financial statement 1 year after University

DETAILS	£
Income	
Salary (after tax)	1,000.00
Total Income	**1,000.00**
Expenditure	
Rent	275.00
Savings fund 10%	100.00
Investment fund 10%	100.00
Car	90.00
Loans & Credit cards	0.00
Utilities	150.00
Food	125.00
Fun & Entertainment	90.00
One-off expense fund	70.00
Total Expenditure	**1,000.00**
Profit / (Loss)	**0.00**

As we can see in the table, Adam has continued to stick with his budget and is still living the frugal lifestyle. Adam now has over £1,200 in savings (£100 × 12months) and £1,200 in investment fund
(£100 × 12months).

We can clearly see Adam's savings and investment columns are growing. They may not be growing as quickly as he wants, but growing investments can take time.

One of his main goals through this whole process is to ensure he has saved up at least three to six months of his monthly

EXPENSES. The reason Adam is doing this is, should any unforeseen circumstance arise like a job loss, six months savings is hopefully more than sufficient cover to ensure their bills can be paid until a new job can be found. This also means that the investment money will not need to be touched and can continue to grow.

The table over the page is looking good, Adam has more than accumulated six months of living expenses in savings and decided to downsize his savings section to 3% per month instead of the original 10%. He then takes the remaining 7% out of savings and ploughs this into his INVESTMENT FUND. 17% of his monthly salary is now going into investments.

Adam's monthly financial statement 5 years after University

DETAILS	£
Income	
Salary (after tax)	1,000.00
Investment income	350.00
Total income	**1,350.00**
Expenditure	
Rent	275.00
Savings fund 3%	41.00
Investment fund 17%	230.00
Car	90.00
Utilities	150.00
Food	125.00
Fun & Entertainment	90.00
One-off expense fund	95.00
Total expenditure	**1,096.00**
Profit	**254.00**

The income and expenses statement shows Adam's perseverance is paying off. Adam has an investment income of £350 on top of his salary, bringing his total income to £1,350. He was able to generate this investment income from investing money from his investment fund. Adam also has a **PROFIT** of **£254**, which he reinvests into his investments.

Looking at this scenario, Adam is wise to do this as his main goal is to become rich, and in order to achieve that, more money is always needed in the investment fund. He feels quite comfortable in reducing the amount as his savings account is quite healthy and can cover the family for more than six months of their living expenses. If Adam's goal was similar to Sally's then he could have used his savings for paying off the MORTGAGE or buying a new car. But Adam has other plans.

We can also see that his investment INCOME is growing. Adam has made a few investments and they are starting to pay off. The money is slowly trickling in, but coming in it is. Hopefully soon we will see this money grow EXPONENTIALLY.

Adam's monthly expense breakdown (including profit)
10 years after leaving University

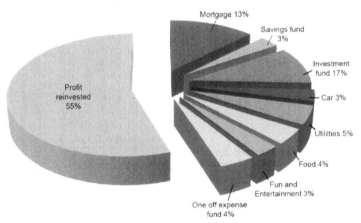

Wow! The profit reinvested is huge at 55%. Adam's game plan of becoming wealthy is working out and his investments are compounding as can be seen with his percentage of profit compared to previous tables.

Adam's monthly financial statement 10 years after University

DETAILS	£
Income	
Salary (after tax)	0.00
Investment income	3,500.00
Total income	**3,500.00**
Expenditure	
Mortgage	450.00
Savings fund 3%	105.00
Investment fund 17%	595.00
Car	110.00
Utilities	175.00
Food	140.00
Fun & Entertainment	140.00
One-off expense fund 4%	140.00
Total expenditure	**1,855.00**
Profit	**1,645.00**

Adam's investment plan is really paying off and now he is earning three and a half times his previous salary. Adam is definitely making headways in becoming wealthy, as we can see from this income and expense statement. He also has a healthy amount of money in savings.

Ten years have come and gone and Adam is on his way to being rich. Let's analyse the table above: his finances are looking really good. His savings have continued to grow, allowing him to buy a new car with cash. This means he has not had to touch any of his investment income, which is being used solely for wealth creation.

The ventures Adam has invested his money in are bringing in a handsome CASH FLOW return monthly. He no longer needs to work for *Computer Express* and his income is now solely being generated from his investments. With at least three to four times his salary coming in on a monthly basis, I would say Adam is definitely on his way to being wealthy. He is achieving his goal of wealth creation, and this can clearly be seen when he compares his ten-year plan, written so long ago with what is actually happening in reality today.

My 10-year wealth creation plan:

10-year goal

Generate enough earnings (income) from my investments so that I can resign from my full-time job and not have to go back to paid work – I can work for myself.

Have a very healthy Savings Account with more than six months living expenses saved.

Be able to enjoy the proceeds from my investments e.g. holidays, a new car, a lovely house and dining at the best restaurants regularly.

Strategy

10% of my salary goes to savings and another 10% of my salary goes towards investments.

First 3 years

- Have as savings three to six months living expenses (will keep this in a savings account).
- Have enough money saved as investments before investing.
- Live off the remaining 80% of salary even if it means living very frugally.

5 years

- Continue saving.
- Have money invested in a few projects, may take time for these investments to bring in a return.

10 years

- Investments to generate good returns (income).
- Have a healthy savings balance in the bank account.
- Able to leave my job because my other income can support my family and me.

15 years after University

Adam's monthly financial statement 15 years after University

DETAILS	£
Income	
Salary (after tax)	0.00
Investment income	7,500.00
Total income	**7,500.00**
Expenditure	
Mortgage	500.00
Savings fund 3%	225.00
Investment fund 10%	750.00
Car	200.00
Utilities	200.00
Food	150.00
Fun & Entertainment	300.00
One-off expense fund 4%	300.00
Total expenditure	**2,625.00**
Profit	**4,875.00**

Do I need to say more? Adam's financial game plan has paid off. We just need to look at the table above to see his initial frugal lifestyle has paid off and now he can enjoy his investments.

Adam is living the good life! All the years of hard work, sacrifice and focus have paid off. He is now running several successful businesses that are generating healthy cash flow. These days, Adam spends his time between these business ventures, overseeing that they are running efficiently. He has gained extensive knowledge in small businesses and partnerships and because of this he is able to invest in quite a few successful deals. This could have only come through years of experience, which he gained when he made some bad investments and some good investments.

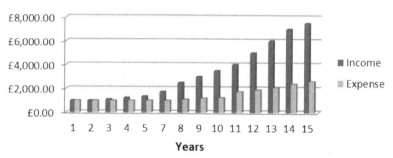

Adam's income & expense analysis over a 15 year period

Adam's income is much greater than his expenses when we look at this diagram. This is a pictorial representation of wealth compounding.

Adam has clearly chosen to go down the route of investing in businesses, be it his own business or investing in an already existing one. Even though he was interested in building wealth, he was more inclined to stay away from the speculating side of investing and was not too interested in rapid growth, preferring to see the money grow significantly over time. It did take Adam some time to reach his target; ten to fifteen years to be exact. However, Adam also learnt some valuable lessons along the way, which he knows will help him to continue achieving success. This was the path Adam decided upon.

As I have said from the beginning, this book is not about how to invest or what to invest in, but more about having a plan and giving you different ideas of what your plan can look like. Adam could have gone down the route of investing in the shares or bonds market, investing in the property market or speculating in so-called 'riskier' vehicles, but he chose to invest in business. If you decide to invest as part of your game plan then I would say it is up to you to decide what form of investment best suits you and what level of risk you are willing to take. The main point to bear in mind is that **Adam was prepared for the risk**. He had a handsome savings balance and was able to pay his expenses comfortably at the end of each month. He was prepared to invest and because of the plan he already had in place and the peace of mind that comes with it, he was also able to make wise decisions on his investment choices. I do believe that if Adam did not have such a plan in place, he could have ended up gambling with his money by making unwise choices in his desperation to EARN some form of income or to generate money.

Definition of compounding for making wealth

COMPOUNDING

The ability of an ASSET to generate earnings. These earnings are then reinvested in order to generate their own earnings.

COMPOUNDING here refers to generating earnings from previous earnings such as interest on interest. This is the principle Adam used to make his wealth. He reinvested his earnings into his investments, which after a time multiplied into wealth.

Therefore, we can see compounding working both ways. As we saw in Brad's story, it worked against him when he **owed** interest and ended up paying interest on top of interest; but here Adam's has used compounding to his advantage and he **receives** interest on top of interest amongst his other earnings.

Defining wealth

> **WEALTH**
>
> The Oxford English Dictionary defines wealth as 'Possessing well-being, being happy, comfortable, or having an abundance of valuable possessions or money'.

I believe wealth is what you make of it as an individual. There is no hard and fast rule. It depends on the goals you set out for yourself as an individual when you think about wealth creation. It could be being debt free, with your mortgage and car paid off. If this is what gives you comfort and peace of mind then you are wealthy. It can also be the other extreme: the lavish lifestyle, having many possessions: cars, an aeroplane, having many properties and shopping at all the best shops, the interpretation most of us as individuals have been taught to think about when defining wealth. This means having an abundance of money to do all these things.

Most people want the latter mentioned above but do not want to put in the hard work and sacrifice to get there. Not all of us are called to be wealthy, but that does not mean we should be careless with our finances and resources (including our time and effort).

I would challenge you to define what wealth means to you. It can mean many different things to many different people. Let's try to use the definition of well-being and comfort, and not the unattainable 'pie in the sky' scenario. Goals must be realistic along with optimistic. To me this is what true wealth is all about: it is not about the fancy cars and big houses, it is more about the peace of mind and comfort that comes from handling your finances wisely.

I believe both Sally and Adam are wealthy people based on the comfort and peace of mind they have achieved. On the outside, Adam's situation may look the part more but Sally has no debt, her house and car are paid off in full, she continues to have good savings and enjoys a lovely family holiday every year. After eighteen years, Sally's savings are such that she can think about buying a second property to have as rental income for when she retires. Therefore, I would put Sally in the wealthy category. Remember wealth is what you make of it.

I would like to give some advice here: **it is crucial that you have a plan**. A one-year, five-year and ten-year plan would be ideal. If you do not currently have a plan and have never thought about it, a five-year or ten-year plan can seem daunting. At least start off with a one-year plan.

If you do not plan for your finances, then your finances will plan for you and the result may not be a good plan. Most of the time it is not. Planning gives you focus and can help with the determination you will need to reach your goal.

I would especially recommend this for individuals in their late teens or early twenties who are now starting off on their financial road. We live in a new economic climate where we need to be very careful with our resources. This is another of the main reasons I wrote this book: to inspire younger generations to have a good financial plan and not follow in the footsteps of prior generations or society as Brad did.

My husband and I have been following the 'wealth and savings' plan for the last four years. When we first got married we did not have a goal for our finances; it did not even enter our heads to have a plan. Our income was meeting our expenditure and we were able to save regularly. There was no routine to our savings and it would differ on a month to month basis. Both my husband and I are quite disciplined with money, but we soon realised not having a solid plan with specific goals was harming us financially. I started reading quite a lot of books on personal finances and attended courses. This, coupled with my accounting experience, gave us the head start we needed. I realised from the knowledge I had gained over the years that actually putting a financial game plan into action was the best course to take. It wasn't that my husband and I were bad with our finances; it was more we did not have a strategy, so therefore financially we were drifting. As soon as my husband and I put a plan into place we started noticing a massive improvement in our finances. Our savings suddenly had a particular purpose and we started putting money away specifically for investment purposes. We deliberately applied the 10% rule for both our savings and investments and lived off the remaining of the income.

Adam's lifestyle is an example of wealth creation and one that a lot of people who want to accumulate wealth follow. Adam wanted to become wealthy and had set himself difficult goals that would call for extreme discipline. We do not all need to follow in Adam's footsteps, but if we understand the principles of what Adam did then we can apply and adapt the principles to meet our own specific needs and desires.

CHAPTER SUMMARY

What is **your** definition of WEALTH?

Do you want to create this wealth? (Not everyone wants to create wealth or wants the sacrifice it will entail.) If so, be specific and realistic when setting your goals.

Adam had a FINANCIAL GAME PLAN, which included a 10% each for his SAVINGS and for INVESTMENTS; he then lived off the remaining 80% of his salary. What is your financial game plan?

Ask yourself:

1. How much money do I need to have saved in the **INVESTMENT FUND** before I can start investing?

2. How long in months or years do I need to save money before I can start?

3. How long would it realistically take me to get there?

Start thinking about OPPORTUNITIES to invest in.

Do some studies or research before investing in an opportunity! Remember Adam's early days.

Train your eyes to look out for investment opportunities.

Learn from other peoples mistakes. Take advice from people in the know. However, just because they know or have experience doesn't mean the advice they give is good. It is imperative that you do your own homework as well.

ACTION PLAN
What Do We Do Now?

I hope you have enjoyed the previous chapters about debt, breakeven, savings and wealth, and have come away with a wealth of knowledge and information that you will take and put into practice. It is one thing to have read the chapters; it is another thing to put what has been learnt into practice. What I have realised with myself, and what you may realise, is that many things will come into your life to distract you. You may think 'I do not have the time right now' or 'I will do it tomorrow', only to realise that tomorrow has become the next day and the next day until you realise that time has gone and some of the information from this book is no longer as fresh in your memory. This then makes it easy not to be bothered and you end up having no FINANCIAL GAME PLAN in place. I know because it has happened to me in the past.

The cares of life come in and the best of intentions can sometimes go straight out the window. I am saying to you right now, you must be bothered. This is money you have worked very hard for: every minute, every hour, day in, day out, year in, year out. You go to work, sometimes in extreme weather conditions, sometimes working through lunch, even holidays, sometimes at the expense of spending quality time with your family. Even with today's depressing economic climate you work longer and harder because you are scared of losing your job. Time passes and so do your finances, and if you don't keep your eye on them you find them filtering through your hands and disappearing into the unknown.

It is now time to take charge: to find out where your money goes, what you spend it on, to think how you are going to make it grow; and to have some sort of strategy.

I won't lie to you, this will take work and effort – if you are working and you EARN an income then you will need to know how to handle your money. If you think you need further help then there are budgeting courses, or maybe get a friend who is good at finances to give you some pointers, or ask someone to set up a basic spreadsheet for you. Just please do not leave your finances alone. As we have seen, this is where the pain and heartache creeps in. Badly handled finances can break up relationships, family, friends and work colleagues, and in extreme situations can even mean you lose your home, as we saw with Brad. You cannot afford to leave your finances alone.

Close your eyes and picture yourself five years from now, ten years from now and even twenty years from now. If you continue on your normal course of action with your finances what does your future look like? Does it look like Brad's story, Jennifer's story, Sally's story or Adam's story? I urge you to do this task: picture your life in the future with the current way you handle your finances and then picture your future if you were to put some of these new goals into place. There is a saying that "a picture paints a thousand words". Let your imagination paint those thousand words, good or bad, of what your finances would really look like if you continue down your present course of action. Keep that picture in your mind. Let it be your motivating force to get your finances in order. They are a big part of your life. They are what you worked so hard for.

If you think getting your finances in order is going to be too hard and you don't know where to start, start with the basics:

- Write up a list of all your INCOME (any money that comes in e.g. salary, government benefits if you receive any etc).

- Write up a list of all your EXPENSES (what you spend money on).

You will need to spend some time getting this right. When I

say write up a list of all your expenses, I mean EVERYTHING. Include daily (e.g. lunch and pocket money) weekly (weekly travel expenses) monthly (utility bills, rent or MORTGAGE, student LOAN) quarterly (telephone bills, television licence) and yearly costs (e.g. insurance costs and car maintenance costs). It is imperative that you give this the attention it deserves. If you have a partner I would recommend doing this exercise with this person. The main point of this exercise is to leave no stone unturned. Look at the examples I have given in the chapters for a format to use and for a possible list of expenses. All households are different, therefore you must make the spreadsheet relevant to you and the costs you have or incur. Please also refer to the blank income and expense sheet at the end of this chapter which you can use to plot your figures.

Find out if you are in a DEBT situation like Brad. If you are in a BREAKEVEN position (where income equals expenditure), have you BUDGETED for a RAINY DAY FUND for unexpected situations? You do not want to be left in the dark like Jennifer. Or you may realise that your finances are not as bad as you thought they were and you have room for SAVINGS, or better yet for both savings and INVESTMENTS.

The reason I say that your finances may be much better than you expected is simply because I have done this exercise of writing up income and expenses with quite a few individuals who had never done this before and on rare occasions we have found things to be more positive than we initially thought.

Some people were really scared to take a look at their finances. In fact, they did not know how to do this exercise and came to me for help. When we got into their finances I could see their faces start to light up because they were now realising that things were not as gloomy as they imagined. However, I do not want to give you any false illusion that this will happen to you. In most cases, when someone hasn't taken the time to understand their finances or has hidden from them, the reality is usually not pleasant. Unfortunately, I have had these situations also. They have often led to many tears being shed by these individuals. However, once they start sorting things out they knew they were on the right track, and today I can say a lot of them are much better off for it.

After you have ascertained which situation you fall into (debt, breakeven, savings or WEALTH creation) then this is where you need to start defining your financial game plan.

If you have found yourself in debt and are wondering what to do about it, please refer to my debt chapter for some useful hints. Look at ways and means you can reduce your spending. Try downsizing where you live, cut out certain luxuries you have. If you are finding it hard to see where to find savings then visit a professional or a charity that specialises in this area. They may see things you did not. If you need further help then please do read up on books relevant to getting out of debt. The main thing at this time is to start preparing a plan for your finances. This game plan may be for getting out of debt by a certain date and after that you can make a new one that can concentrate on creating savings or wealth. It is really up to you what your approach is going to look like.

The same criteria apply in order to breakeven, develop savings or build wealth. Most people will not have even thought of the wealth building. I would also like to point out that the 10% principle applied to both savings and wealth creating is not a hard and fast rule, it is a guideline only. This amount is the one usually recommended by FINANCIAL ADVISORS but you do not have to follow it. You can come up with your own plan; if you can only afford to save 5% on a monthly basis then that is fine too, as long as you have budgeted for those ONE-OFF EXPENSES. I would recommend that you aim to save a minimum of 2% of your monthly income rather than none at all. A lot of people have used the 10% rule for their savings and also for building wealth and it has worked for them; therefore it does have a proven track record. However, I would like to stress that each person has unique circumstances and these should be taken into consideration.

Income & expenses spreadsheet template

NB For "Other Charges", make sure you list each item individually.

CATEGORY	MONTHLY BUDGET AMOUNT
INCOME:	
Wages/ Salary after tax	
Bonus	
Benefits (List individually)	
Any Other Income	
Total INCOME:	
EXPENSES:	
HOME:	
Mortgage or Rent	
Building Insurance	
Contents Insurance	
Property Taxes (Council Tax, House Tax)	
Service Charges	
Other Home Charges	
Total HOME:	
UTILITIES:	
Electricity	
Gas	
Water	
TV Licence	
Satellite/Cable	
Telephone (Landline, Mobile)	
Broadband	

Other Utilities	
Total UTILITIES:	
FOOD:	
Groceries	
Lunches, Snacks etc	
Meals out, Takeaways	
Other Food	
Total FOOD:	
TRANSPORTATION:	
Car Payments	
Insurance	
Tax	
Servicing / MOT	
Other Transportation (Bus, Tube, Train etc)	
Total TRANSPORTATION:	
DEBT PAYMENTS:	
Credit Cards	
Store Cards	
Bank Loan	
Hire Purchase	
Other Loans	
Total DEBT REPAYMENTS:	
ENTERTAINMENT:	
Vacations	
Memberships (Gym, Golf, DVD clubs etc)	
Subscriptions (Magazines, Newspapers	

Friends and Family Time (Activities etc)	
Children's Activities (Scouts, Ballet, Drama etc)	
Total ENTERTAINMENT:	
ONE-OFF EXPENSES:	
Grooming (Haircuts, Nail Bar etc)	
Gifts/Donations	
Household Item Replacements	
Other Expenses	
Total ONE-OFF EXPENSES:	
INVESTMENTS/SAVINGS:	
Savings (ISAs, Savings Accounts etc)	
University/College Savings Funds	
Holiday Savings Funds	
Investments (ISAs, Stocks, Bonds etc)	
Total INVESTMENTS/SAVINGS:	
OTHER UNSPECIFIED EXPENSES	
List anything not mentioned above e.g. Pension	
Total OTHER EXPENSES:	
TOTAL INVESTMENTS AND EXPENSES	
PROFIT OR LOSS (TOTAL INCOME – TOTAL EXPENSES)	

107

CHAPTER SUMMARY

Action Time

The knowledge gained from the above chapters should be applied to your personal financial information or position. It is practice time and it is important to avoid distractions that will take you away from doing this. *Yes the distractions do come!*

You need to put in time and effort. Are you up for the challenge?

It is always good to start with the basics:

1. Take the time to know and list **ALL** your INCOME and EXPENSES.

2. Use the 'blank income and expense sheet' included in this chapter as your guide.

It is good to identify which position you fall into: debt, breakeven, savings or wealth. If you have both savings and debt, the one with the greater amount will tell you which category you fall into.

If you are finding it hard doing this exercise, ask someone professional for help or visit organisations that specialise in this area. Many charities out there exist to help individuals in this area.

Badly handled finances can break up relationships, family, friends and colleagues and can even mean you lose your home.

FOOLPROOF YOUR GAME PLAN

Brad, Jennifer, Sally and Adam Demystified

Over the last few chapters, we have read about our four friends, Brad, Jennifer, Sally and Adam. We looked at their SAVINGS and spending habits and how this affected their lives, their family lives and their lifestyles. This chapter will now go into analysing Brad's, Jennifer's, Sally's and Adam's financial approaches. You will learn important tips on how to examine your BUDGET and, more importantly, how to get your budget process right.

I know that there are a lot of people who do not like figures, and like looking at them in spreadsheets and graphs even less. This can be a total turn-off for many people. I hope you will be pleasantly surprised by how user-friendly the information is and how pain-free the process is, especially when you walk away with information that will assist you in having a foolproof plan.

Let's start with analysing these four individuals' INCOME and EXPENSES side by side. We will look at their first salary straight after university. Remember, Brad, Jennifer, Sally and Adam all have the same job, all worked for the same company, with the same salary of £1,000 and at the same time. We are using the average monthly figures.

Monthly financial statement after University

DETAILS	£			
	Brad	**Jennifer**	**Sally**	**Adam**
Income	1,000.00	1,000.00	1,000.00	1,000.00
Expenditure	1,200.00	1,000.00	1,000.00	1,000.00
Profit / (Loss)	**(200.00)**	**0.00**	**0.00**	**0.00**

We now know the story. The table shows that they are all earning the same income of £1,000. We can also see that Brad is the only one who is spending more than he is earning on a monthly basis, with an average loss of £200. Jennifer, Sally and Adam are all keeping within their earnings.

They are all now out of university and so they are also spending more freely at this time in their lives because they do not have a MORTGAGE or family responsibilities e.g. a husband/wife or children.

I do believe they should enjoy themselves with a treat or two but one must know there is a fine line between that and getting into DEBT, as we can see with Brad and his loss position.

Analysis of spending habits on non core items after University

	Car	Loans & credit cards	Fun & entertainment	Percentage
Brad	200.00	195.00	200.00	60%
Jennifer	150.00	75.00	175.00	40%
Sally	110.00	50.00	135.00	30%
Adam	90.00	0.00	90.00	18%

For the 'percentage' column, my calculations for this section using Brad:

```
        £200 (Car)
        £195 (Loans & Credit cards)
    +   £200 (Fun & Entertainment)
        £595 (Total cost)
```

60% =   £595 (Total cost above)   0.595 × 100 (percentage) = 59.5%
    +   £1,000 (Salary)   (rounded to 60% for ease of understanding)
        0.595

This shows the percentage of expenditure used on Brad's non-core items.

As I said we saw that Brad had a monthly loss of £200 and when we look at the diagram above we can see the reason why. A total of 60% of his £1,000 salary was going towards non-core items; these are not necessities like food and rent. 60% of his salary is quite a lot to be spending on these items especially when we compare it to Jennifer's 40%, Sally's 30% and

Adam's very small 18%. Brad is really enjoying spending maybe a bit too much while Adam is spending quite frugally, but still seems to be enjoying life a little bit.

I would like to point out that in the above table 'Analysis of spending habits on non-core items straight after university' I have put CAR COSTS into this table because it was not an essential (necessary) cost for our four individuals. They each have other transportation alternatives they can use. For some people reading this book 'car cost' can be a core expense. If, for example, it were your only way of getting to and from work then factoring this cost as a priority core cost would be important for you.

5 years after University

Monthly financial statement 5 years after University

DETAILS	£			
	Brad	**Jennifer**	**Sally**	**Adam**
Income	1,000.00	1,000.00	1,000.00	1,350.00
Expenditure	1,770.00	1,150.00	1,000.00	1,096.00
Profit / (Loss)	**(770.00)**	**(150.00)**	**0.00**	**254.00**

We can see here how Brad's debt has compounded, leaving him with a MONTHLY loss of £770. As Jennifer hasn't put in a contingency for her unexpected costs, she is now in debt too. Sally is on target with her budgeting, and Adam is beginning to make a nice profit.

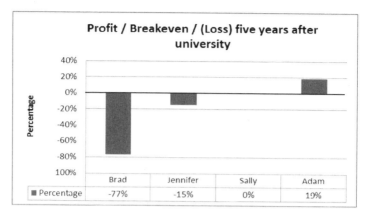

Breakeven position is at '0', which is where Sally is. Any figure beneath that line is a loss, where Brad and Jennifer are, and any figure above that line is a profit, where Adam is.

Looking at their situation five years on shows a more realistic picture of what happens if they carry on with their spending and savings habits. Brad is making a really large loss of 77% of his income on a MONTHLY basis. Jennifer had the real shock as she also has a monthly average debt of 15%. Sally is getting her budget process right with no loss and Adam is making a profit 19% of his total monthly income.

We must remember that:

- Brad did not have a financial strategy. Therefore he did not have a budget in place for his income, which is why he is now in a 'Loss' position.

- Although Jennifer did have a FINANCIAL PLAN, her budget process of a BREAKEVEN position was not foolproof enough, and now she too is actually in a 'Loss' situation.

113

- Sally's financial line of attack of paying off her mortgage in ten to fifteen years from the date of purchase is working. So far she seems to be getting her budgeting right.

- Adam had a very frugal budget for accomplishing his financial goal, which is a ten-year plan. Up to now it seems to be working, putting him in a 'Profit' situation.

Analysis of spending habits 5 years after University

	Mortgage/ Rent	Loans & credit cards	Fun & entertainment
Brad	55%	42%	21%
Jennifer	40%	11%	10%
Sally	40%	0%	6%
Adam	27%	0%	9%

This table shows each section as a percentage of their whole income.

Mortgage/Rent

If we remember, Brad bought a beautiful house in an expensive neighbourhood. As we can see with his monthly mortgage payment at 55% of his income, more than half of his monthly income is going towards his mortgage. This is quite a large amount. Adam, on the other hand, is still renting, with only 28%, or roughly a quarter of his £1,000 income, going towards his rent. He has a strategy in place for getting wealthy and needs as much income to INVEST in his plan as he can get, hence his frugal lifestyle. Both Jennifer and Sally have allocated

40% to their mortgage; but we must remember that Sally has a goal to pay off her mortgage in ten to fifteen years and so is paying more to this section to clear this mortgage debt faster and hence her 40% expense.

Loans & Credit cards

Brad is paying a monthly amount of £420, or 42% on LOANS and CREDIT CARDS. This is nearly half of his income. We must also remember that more than half his income is already going towards his mortgage. That leaves him with very little, or no income remaining for anything else at the end of the month. Jennifer also has a monthly charge of 11% in loans and credit cards when in fact she never wanted any debt and thought she had worked towards this goal. Sally and Adam have stayed away from loans and credit cards and therefore have 0% balances in this section. Remember Sally paid off her small student loan some time back and has not added to this section since, and Adam never had a student loan.

Fun & Entertainment

This section tells us a lot about what our four friends view as important. Brad is spending 21% of his income on having a good time. But wait! His income is already spent on 'Mortgage' and 'Loans and Credit Cards'. Brad has no choice but to add this expense to his ever growing debt. Brad is living way beyond his means. Jennifer is spending 10% on FUN AND

ENTERTAINMENT, but has some debt also. If she knew she did not want debt she could have cut back on this cost to avoid getting into this position. Sally and Adam have allocated 6% and 9% respectively. These percentages seem reasonable in context of their financial game plan. I do believe as individuals we must always section out part of our salary for fun and entertainment. I have always done this in my personal budget and I view this as extremely important as it helps me put aside time for fun activities and socialising with friends and family. Nevertheless I must add that this expense be a reasonable portion of our salary and not an excessive one leading to debt, as we see with Brad.

Analysing saving habits

Analysis of funds 5 years after University

	One-off expense Fund	Savings Fund	Investment Fund
Brad	0%	0%	0%
Jennifer	0%	0%	0%
Sally	7%	10%	0%
Adam	10%	4%	23%

Upon looking at the above table, both Brad and Jennifer have no saving habits with 0% in all three columns. This is why Brad's situation is so very bad and Jennifer's is not looking good.

Both Sally and Adam know the importance of savings. Breaking it down into different sections, we can see from the table that Sally has money in both her ONE-OFF EXPENSE FUND and SAVINGS FUND. Adam is also transferring money to both these sections, as well as his INVESTMENT FUND. By looking at their savings habits, we can instantly tell who has a strategy, who is budgeting responsibly and who is not.

We will now jump seventeen years after university and analyse Brad and Adam's positions.

Brad and Adam's financial statement 17 years after University

DETAILS	Brad	Adam
Income		
Salary (after tax)	1,300.00	0.00
Investment income	0.00	9,000.00
Total income	**1,300.00**	**9,000.00**
Expenditure		
Mortgage	350.00	500.00
Savings fund	60.00	270.00
Investment fund	0.00	900.00
Car	125.00	200.00
Loans & Credit cards	350.00	0.00
Utilities	165.00	200.00
Food	150.00	150.00
Fun & Entertainment	50.00	300.00
One-off expense fund	50.00	360.00
Total expenditure	**1,300.00**	**2,880.00**
Profit	**0.00**	**6,120.00**

I have put the full budget analysis in to give you a complete picture of what things look like after seventeen years. Seventeen years is quite a long time and things are definitely looking better for Brad now, and very good for Adam. I know a lot of us want to know what happens to Brad.

Brad

Good news! Brad has now cleared the majority of his debts. However, this took seven years, and he still has to pay some off. His loan and credit card payments are still there, but they are not as large as they were previously. Brad recently got a better paying job, assisting him to pay off his debts quicker, and allowing him to give up his weekend job. It also meant that he could buy a small house in an affordable neighbourhood. He has money in both his one-off expense fund and savings fund. Brad and his family now have peace of mind, but this came at a huge price and they are living a frugal but peaceful lifestyle with the extravagant ways of the past being just a memory. The main priority for them is to have a solid financial strategy and avoid the trouble they previously found themselves in.

Adam

Adam's WEALTH just keeps COMPOUNDING. We can see this by just looking at his income and expenses: he has a profit of £6,120 per month; that is a very large figure. His financial approach has paid off and continues to do so.

What a story!

Recommendations

In Sally's *Savings* chapter we looked at the FIXED RULE approach verses the PERCENTAGE RULE. To recap:

1. Applying a fixed monetary amount to your monthly income example saving £50 every month.

OR

2. Applying a percentage (%) of your monthly income to savings like the example used with Sally saving 10% of her monthly income.

This principle can be applied to the majority of our costs.

- It would be good for you to look at your monthly expenses and find out what percentages they represent of your monthly income. Let this be the guide to help you see where the majority of your spending is going and what you actually want, as we did when analysing our four friends.

- Think about what your ideal expense percentages look like, especially if you are about to buy a property or a car. See how much of the monthly payment will be eating into your income and ask yourself those important questions:
    - is this too large a portion of my income?
    - is this going to take me into debt or make me stressed?

If you already have a house or car, but it eats up a large

portion of your income leaving you stressed, look at what adjustments you can make: maybe selling the house or car. I know some of you may not like that idea, but these are hard questions you need to ask yourself to remove some of that stress.

- You can apply the FIXED RULE APPROACH or the PERCENTAGE RULE interchangeably to different sections of your expenses. You may want to use the percentage rule for your one-off expenses fund, your savings fund or your investment fund. Alternatively, you could use the fixed approach to some funds and the percentage rule for others. It really depends what works best for you. Ask yourself what is comfortable to work with.

I did not want to give fixed amounts or percentages on specific categories e.g. mortgages etc. The reason for this is we are all individuals and we all have different desires. No two budgets look the same, even if we EARN the same amount of money, as we clearly saw with our four friends.

Good debt vs. bad debt – the illusion continued

We briefly touched upon this topic way back in the *Debt Analysis: stressed and depressed* chapter. To reiterate, it said that debt is debt and it is up to the individual as to whether it is a problem or not. It also stated that some debts are obviously considered good, e.g. a mortgage to buy a house or a student loan to attend university. But too often buying a home or getting a degree is a starting point for getting into debt rather than a starting point for being good financial stewards.

I am sure you have gathered that I am no advocator of debt. I have seen too many times what debt can do to an individual, to families, to businesses and even to countries, and these situations have not been pleasant. Nevertheless, for this particular part of the book I put aside my personal biases about debt and have included a section that will hopefully open your eyes to the 'Good debt/Bad debt' discussion, and also help you foolproof your financial planning. I hope it brings illumination and understanding about debt: how to use it, when to use it, why you should use it and whether you should use it at all.

We will be using our four friends and their financial situations five years after leaving university to explain this. Let us start with Brad.

Brad

We know that five years after university Brad was spending more than his monthly earnings. This was happening on a continuous basis and Brad did not seem to realise or care. He had no savings, he could not even afford to save and he already had a lot of debt to his name, possibly affecting his CREDIT HISTORY and rating. Therefore, from this analysis, there seemed to be no purpose to Brad's debt and it looks uncontrollable. I am sure you will agree Brad definitely falls into the BAD debt category.

Jennifer

Jennifer's situation is slightly different to Brad. Jennifer did not want debt but did not budget for unexpected costs, leading her to acquire unnecessary debt five years after university. On top of that, Jennifer had no savings, but her CREDIT SCORE and credit history was okay because her debt amount was manageable and definitely not out of control as we saw with Brad. Unfortunately, Jennifer's debt still falls under BAD debt, due to the simple fact that it was unplanned. She was spending more than she earned and she had neither savings nor a plan to get out of debt.

Sally

We have all read that Sally had a plan to purchase her own home but would need to take out a mortgage in order to do so. Sally saw this mortgage as a GOOD debt. Why?

1. Sally had a purpose for borrowing – owning her own home.

2. Sally was able to meet all her monthly financial obligations along with her mortgage payments without getting into unnecessary extra debt as Brad and Jennifer did.

3. She kept a good financial history and record allowing her to borrow on positive terms and with good INTEREST RATES from a financial institution.

4. Sally had a healthy SAVINGS account.

Sally was prepared for this debt. This debt could have been for a car or for a holiday, but the main thing is that Sally was equipped for it. In this case we called this debt GOOD.

Adam

Adam wanted to accumulate wealth, and five years down the line he was not doing too badly in achieving this endeavour. Adam wanted to do this with no debt, or as little as possible.

Let's use an example to illustrate this point. A great investment OPPORTUNITY comes Adam's way. Unfortunately he does not have sufficient capital for this investment but he has done his homework and is nearly 100% certain the investment will prove profitable. What is Adam to do?

In this case, if Adam decides to borrow the additional money needed then:

1. He has a plan for this loan – a probable good investment.

2. He can take out this loan and still be able to meet all his monthly financial obligations, including this monthly loan repayment.

3. He has an exceptionally good credit history and credit score and therefore is able to command a good rate from lending institutions.

4. Adam still has his savings 'peace of mind' money .

Now Adam is taking a RISK here because he is using this loan to invest. BUT, and I say a huge BUT, he is prepared for it. All we need to do is look at his financial situation to gather this. I would therefore have no choice but to call this GOOD debt. Adam would be in control of this debt rather than this debt being in control of him. Even if Adam was to lose all the money he put into this investment; both his personal investment money and the loan money through investing in this risk, by using his other income and savings, he could still **pay all his monthly bills and have peace of mind at the end of it.**

Debt conclusion

I hope this section brings clarity and enlightenment on debt. I know there are many situations where the above may not necessarily apply. One example that comes to mind would be taking out a loan to get a degree or to tide a person over as they study. These individuals most of the times would not have savings or a credit history because they may have come straight out of the school system. Situations like these are very common and most of the times we have our parents or government facilities to fall back on. My main objective here is to show that although going to university or studying is great, please do not let it lull you into a false illusion that the debt is not there. It is, and therefore whatever plan you put in place you must remember that you are already starting your journey with a certain level of debt. Whether it is Good, Bad or In-between is your choice.

CHAPTER SUMMARY

Foolproof Approach

Make sure:

1. You have a plan.

2. It is a sensible strategy.

3. It fits in with the lifestyle you want without getting into senseless debt.

4. You are able to stick with the plan. This is very important. There is no sense in making a BUDGET you cannot stick with. Set a realistic budget; not everyone can do what Adam did.

Then there is the bonus of peace of mind. This is fundamental to the whole foolproof process.

CHAPTER SUMMARY continued

Good debt/Bad debt

Questions to ask yourself:

1. Is there a purpose for borrowing?

2. Am I able to meet all my monthly financial obligations including this additional borrowing without getting stressed or into unnecessary debt?

3. Do I have a financial record and history which allows me to borrow on good terms and with good rates from lending institutions?

4. Have I got a healthy SAVINGS balance?

Depending on your answers to these four questions will generally determine which category of debt you fall into though at times it may not always be this black and white.

Well I hope you enjoyed this chapter and you are now armed with some good ammunition for foolproofing your finances.

A NEW WAY OF THINKING
Opportunities & Risks

I had no intention of writing this section, but realised by leaving it out I was probably leaving out one of the best parts of this book. My husband and I present this book in seminar form and I think this is usually the section the audiences get most excited about because they never saw opportunities and risks the way my husband and I present them.

Opportunities

These opportunities sometimes come once in a lifetime. Some people, because they are constantly on the lookout, are able to get them more frequently. I believe if we train ourselves to be on the lookout for such opportunities, they will start coming our way. At the beginning it may seem slow, but as we continue to train our eyes to look for them it becomes easier, as Adam found.

What do I mean by OPPORTUNITIES?

OPPORTUNITIES

In the context of this book, opportunities are openings, occasions or chances to get involved with a great INVESTMENT: business, stock market, property etc.

Opportunities can come in two forms: the first are ones that we as individuals are on the lookout for. We train our eyes and ears to see and hear when they come our way. They could be a business venture, or the chance to buy a property at a fantastic bargain price. The reason we are able to look for and take up such opportunity is because we are prepared. We have made our FINANCIAL PLAN, our CREDIT SCORE is great, we have little or no debt and, most importantly, we have savings for such a time as this. We are then able to easily take up such opportunities when they are presented to us.

If our investment money is not sufficient, because over the years we have been careful with our finances and so have a good financial record, we are able to borrow quite easily and at good rates with our bank or other lending institutions.

The second form of opportunities comes along less often, but when they do come they are a great chance to create WEALTH and grow money. Two examples that come to mind are 1) a stock market crash, or what I term stock market sale, and 2) investing in a ground breaking business or product that is about to be launched on the market. These kinds of situations usually only happens once, twice or three times in a lifetime. I would say this current economic climate is great for an opportunity hunter where there are many bargains to have if one is willing to wait patiently. What do I mean by this? I remember when Lehman Brothers bank went into BANKRUPTCY and along with it came the stock market crash, a lot of people got really scared when they lost quite a bit of money in the stock market, in their PENSION funds and when their stocks and shares investment went down. People were pulling money out of the stock market from every direction. This was a great investment opportunity. With no prior experience investing in stocks and shares, I opened up a trading account and started buying shares in companies. I must stress that my husband and I did have our SAVINGS FUND and our INVESTMENT FUNDS by then. I was financially prepared to play the market, knowing if I lost money in such volatile market conditions I still had my savings. I saw opportunity and took it. I bought shares in some of the big companies we know today at a reduced price. And these were companies with great financial histories. Within months I was then able to sell these shares at a profit. Since this was my first time investing in shares I was a little cautious and did not use a huge portion of my investment fund, but what I did invest brought me a handsome return. As I said, opportunities like this do not come around very often but when they do they are great ways of making money.

It is the same with property. Let's take the American property market as an example. I am sure we are all aware of how far the American property market has fallen in recent years, with property selling at reduced prices in comparison to previous years. This could be a great investment opportunity if someone was to do their proper research and invest in the right type of property, be it for rental or to sell when property prices rise in the future.

I am not saying to suddenly take your money and buy property in America, or go into the stock market when it is crashing. As I have already said, **you must do your own homework beforehand** and ensure you get some expert advice before buying into any of these markets. Remember, investment comes with a certain level of risk involved and you must be prepared to lose this money. No one wants to lose their hard-earned cash, but investments are not the same as savings, which offer safe returns. An investment always comes with risk but, as Adam learnt, the risk **must** be calculated. A certain level of research must be put in first. Do not ever go into an opportunity blindly. You must thoroughly understand what you are putting your money into. This is about making your money work for you. The more prepared you are, the better your investment decisions will be.

Risks

The definition of RISK and how it influences our perceptions of investment and opportunity

This section looks at what 'risk' means within the context of investment, and maybe introduces a new way of thinking regarding investing and investments.

As I previously mentioned, my husband and I have been presenting this book about Brad and Adam in seminar form for some time now in colleges and community centres, and, especially when presenting the Adam section of wealth development, I often get asked one specific question: 'I want high returns but I'm scared of the high risk. What should I do?' I just shake my head to that question as it seems to be so deeply entrenched in our thinking that high risk means greater reward and that low risk means low rewards. I want to clarify or even change that perception.

Before I say anything further I just wanted to reiterate what I have said throughout this book: this book is not about investment advice, nor is it about how to get rich. Instead I am aiming to focus your mind on having a plan for your personal finances, and also maybe alter the way you think about finances.

> **RISK**
>
> The Oxford English Dictionary defines RISK as the possibility of being exposed to danger or loss.

Therefore, we know there is a possibility we can lose our investment money depending on the risk we take. That is why we separate out our savings from our investment fund and we have discussed this in detail in the Adam story chapter *Wealth Analysis*. Hence we know investments come with the risk of losing your investment money when taking up such opportunities.

Nevertheless, we hear these particular phrases in our everyday lives: 'this is a high-risk investment', or 'it is best to put your money in this investment because it is low risk'. Our investment choices are based on this information coming at us from the media, bank and investment houses and, at times, even our FINANCIAL ADVISORS, and we accept it, sometimes without research or question.

I think potentially this is a big mistake. Why? Let me use an analogy to explain what I mean. When we are buying a car or a washing machine we do research, we compare prices, we ask the neighbours what they use and if they find it satisfactory and useful. We tend to speak to more than one person to get a good and healthy viewpoint before buying such items. We sometimes visit more than one store or we check out the reviews about the car or washing machine on the internet. We do not just rush out and buy them without finding out about them first. We all want a car or washing machine that will work for us and we put in the time and effort to get the perfect, or next to perfect, car or washing machine for our particular situation.

Concerning investing, I find many people are the total opposite, and even quite lazy with their investment decisions. Most of us stick to the traditional route of going to our banks or financial advisors to help us make the decisions about where, how and what to invest in, and then leave those financial advisors to sort it all out. It seems that people really do not want the headache of investing. They hand the decision over to an advisor who asks them the million-dollar question: 'How risk-tolerant are you?' My interpretation of this is 'are you interested in HIGH-RISK or LOW-RISK INVESTMENTS?' Based on your answers to this question, the advisor will then give you recommendations on products you should invest in.

What do 'high risk' and 'low risk' really mean, and why do they make us hesitate in making investment decisions? Should it really make us hesitate? This is where knowledge is so important. Remember what I said in the *Opportunity* section: learn to develop your mind to see an opportunity. By developing your thinking to look for opportunities you will also increase your knowledge about them. Let me give you an example of what I am trying to explain. A lot of us believe that investing in the stock market is high risk. However, there are some people who think that investing in the stock market is low risk or as safe as putting money in the bank (if, of course, you know what you are doing). So why is it perceived as high risk for some and low risk for others? It boils down to knowledge: some people are more knowledgeable about the stock market than others. I am not saying to suddenly go out and invest in the stock market because it is low risk. Actually, it can be quite dangerous even to those who do know what they are doing. However, as I explained before, investments are a risk and it depends on your personal knowledge about that INVESTMENT VEHICLE that will make it high or low risk.

That is why I advise individuals who ask me to invest in things they are passionate or knowledgeable about. For example, if you like cars and are quite knowledgeable in that area that may just be **your** investment opportunity. The reason being, because of your knowledge and passion, you will be more likely to keep up-to-date with current information and trends, which will give you an insight into your investments. If we find our investment topic boring we could find it arduous to oversee our investments and therefore less likely to pay as much attention to it – hence the risk!

It is not always best that we stick within the box by having a financial advisor or using our bank products because it is the easiest way to do it. Yes, they are good and have their part to play, but we must remember that we have our part to play also; it is our hard-earned money. It is good to get out of the box and do things that broaden our thinking, like reading this book.

Therefore, I would say a high-risk investment, most of the time, is based on lack of knowledge. When a person is not knowledgeable about an opportunity then it is suddenly high risk. For someone else that same opportunity can be low risk because they may know quite a bit about it. Using their knowledge, they are then able to make a so-called 'high return' on that investment. Remember what I said: a lot of people's perception is that 'high risk' equals 'high return' but to the person in the know this was not a high-risk opportunity, it was actually low risk and brought in a high return. There is also the danger that sometimes a high-risk investment can give a low return.

Bear in mind, there are some high-risk opportunities that no matter how much knowledge you have about them will still be high risk. An example of this would be investing in a first-rate business situated in a very politically unstable country. A good business in an unstable country could be negatively affected by the erratic decisions of the leaders of that country and its economy.

I must leave it at that and point out, before you invest in anything, knowledge about that investment is powerful and can help make the decision between high-risk or low-risk investments that so many people ask me about. Please do not rely solely on your financial advisor for advice. Their advice may be good, but it should be weighed up carefully and you should do some homework yourself. Remember what I said: it is your money and knowledge is power.

CHAPTER SUMMARY

OPPORTUNITIES are openings, occasions or chances to get involved with a great INVESTMENT: business, stock market, property etc. They can come either once in a lifetime or more frequently if we are on the lookout for them. Not everyone knows what an opportunity is because the majority of us are not taught to recognise them. Training ourselves to be on the lookout for opportunities will help us see them when they arrive.

Opportunities arrive in two forms:

1. When we the individual are on the lookout for them.

2. When society places them in front of us e.g. a stock market crash or when property prices have fallen. These sorts of opportunities do not come around very often, maybe once or twice in a lifetime.

Never go into an opportunity without doing homework on it. Blindly taking up an opportunity can be risky.

RISK is the possibility of being exposed to danger or loss, for the context of this book danger or loss in an investment or opportunity.

CHAPTER SUMMARY continued...

High risk/Low risk: what does that really mean? Not every high-return investment is high risk or low-return investment low risk, but society trains us to think so. It is about time we changed our perception and became wise with investments and risks.

Knowledge is key to avoiding or reducing risk. More often than not, the more knowledge you have, the less risk you take, and vice versa.

I recommend visiting a bank or FINANCIAL ADVISOR and possibly investing in the products they offer **BUT** after we have done our own homework. We should also be on the lookout for investment ourselves.

10

DEBUNKING COUNTRIES' FINANCES

Global Analysis

How can the previous chapters apply to countries?

You may be asking why *Global Analysis* is in this book and how is this going to benefit you. There are two main reasons for writing this chapter; firstly that what happens in the global economy affects our personal finances and our FINANCIAL GAME PLAN. We may not realise it but it does impact us. And secondly, that the stories about our four friends and their situations can actually apply to countries as well, believe it or not. I hope that this chapter will open your eyes and bring **clarity** on global economics.

One day I got into a discussion with a well-educated political representative. We spoke about world finances and the current recession taking place in many countries. The debate turned heated and we both had opposing views. We agreed it was important for countries to get their finances under control. Where we disagreed, however, was *HOW*. The other person felt that it was more important to grow an economy by whatever means possible, including taking on more DEBT as a country, rather than reduce a country's DEFICIT. To a certain extent I agreed with her, but only up to the point of growing the economy, not by adding to the deficit or any other means possible. I personally felt it necessary that a country should get their spending under control. She then went on to say that all countries run a deficit and asked therefore what was the problem? When I heard that comment come out of her mouth I was shocked. At that exact moment I realised a lot of people may be under the same impression: that there is nothing wrong with a country running a continuous deficit, and that all countries do this. Not only that, but I believe there are a lot of people under the illusion that personally this is okay. Many people do not realise there are consequences for a country that adopts this policy.

Let's take this further and clarify.

We have analysed the debt, breakeven, savings and wealth sections for individuals in the previous chapters. What isn't so immediately obvious is that these same lessons can be applied to world economies and countries. It really is that simple. I know it is easy to be sometimes deceived into thinking that countries operate by totally different principles to us and that the same rules do not apply. It is sometimes difficult to imagine a country having INCOME and EXPENSES like us. Even though a country's finance system is more complex than an individual's, the same basic principle applies.

A country EARNS income and has expenses. Its income can come from its export industry; from agriculture or manufacturing of goods; or from its services, for example financial services. London is known for its financial services, which generates huge income for the British Government annually. A country also generates income from the TAXES it receives from you and me. For example, in Britain we have Income Tax, National Insurance, and VAT (Valued Added Tax) amongst others. This is just a basic look at how a country can generate income.

A country also has expenses, money it has to pay out in order to run the country. These expenses can be government workers' salaries: – employees who work on behalf of the country, e.g. teachers, police officers, and firefighters to name but a few. Roads, parks, schools, libraries etc. need to be maintained or upgraded. PENSIONS need to be paid to the older population as well as many other expenses. All this costs money, and they are paid from the income generated by the country. This is as basic as it can be to define how a country's finances work. Therefore, if **its income is greater than its expenses then the country is operating with a** SURPLUS or, what we term in this book, SAVINGS. If **a country's expenses are more than its income then it is operating on a deficit,** or what this book calls DEBT. Let's break this down further and put these into the different categories we have read about in previous chapters.

Debt

As we read in the first chapter with our friend Brad, if an individual spends more than they earn then after a while they will accumulate debt. This debt always needs to be repaid. They may need to pay back a bank, building society, family or friend but the money will always need to be paid back, depending on the terms and conditions negotiated before borrowing it.

The same applies to countries – if a country spends more than it earns monthly, yearly or on a continuous basis, then sooner or later the institution or bank that the country borrowed from will ask to be repaid. Today there are a lot of countries that are in this situation. Let's take for example the country I live in: Great Britain. For many years Britain has spent more than the income it has generated. Hence Britain has been running a deficit for quite a few years.

The government now has to make cuts exactly as Brad did. Brad overspent in the good years and had to pay back in the lean years. Many countries, including Britain, overspent in the good years and now the lean years are here and that money needs to be repaid or, as the government phrases it, 'the deficit needs to be reduced'.

There are many people under the illusion that it is okay for a country to run a deficit and continue to do so. It may not seem obvious in the here and now but debt does catch up with a country. It always does. 'Debt' or 'deficit'; it is one and the same thing. Debt is debt, no matter how we phrase it. **The way it catches up with individuals is the same way it catches up with countries; it just takes longer to catch up with countries than it does individuals.** There is only so much debt one can take on before it comes back to bite in the pocket.

A lot of us enjoyed the good days before the economic crash of 2008. CREDIT was easily available and we could walk into a bank and take out a MORTGAGE or a LOAN quite easily. The criteria for getting a loan or mortgage were much easier than they are at present. Today we see a different story: credit (money that is borrowed or not ours) is no longer easily available. It's payback time and, as we saw with Brad having to downsize and take control of his personal finances, we are now living an austere lifestyle. We are seeing lots of job cuts and redundancies, and new jobs are not easily available as Brad experienced. A lot more people are taking part-time jobs because businesses cannot afford full-time positions. More and more people have to go onto government benefits, which the government offers for those who are unemployed or in low income jobs, and even these are being more rigorously monitored than before. A lot of people never thought this would happen to them. We are seeing these situations right before our very eyes today; it is constantly on the news and in the media. It's a dire state of affairs.

Most of us do not understand how this could have happened, wondering how we ever got into such a situation. I hope the debt chapter about Brad helped you to understand how debt can come upon a person or country. It is exactly the same principle. Britain, America, Greece, Portugal, Argentina and so many other countries are in debt. They have, over the years, spent more money than they have earned and it is now time to repay what they have borrowed. To understand how the countries borrow and finance themselves is not for this book, so long as you understand the principle. Many governments today have no choice but to downsize. We are seeing the cuts come in many different forms, in many different countries. Some governments have had no choice but to cut back drastically. This debt problem has been developing for many years, and it is amazing that we did not have to cut back before now. If we had, then at least the problem would not have been so big, or seem so out of control. Think of Brad and his debt situation COMPOUNDING. I guess these countries need to ask themselves 'What were we thinking? What was our financial game plan? Did we even have one?' And last big question:

'Were we only living for the here and now and not thinking about our future generations?' The financial future of the next generation in these countries is sadly already laden with debt.

How can we help our countries in this situation? I personally believe the answer lies in getting our personal finances in order, clearing our personal debts and putting aside money as savings. By not being a financial burden to the system, not needing medical care due to undue stress, which costs money, and by being good stewards we can set examples for others around us, including our governments, to follow. Can you imagine if we got clued up on our finances, became wise on simple financial planning and some of us lobbied governments on the financial policies they set? We could possibly make a positive difference in society. I know this sounds idealistic and a bit unrealistic, but hey, we must start somewhere!

How can we steer a country in the right direction if our own personal lives are a financial mess? Think about it. I know many people will say it was not their fault that their country is in debt and ask why they should have to pay the consequences. If we really looked at Brad's story, or even our own personal money history, we can then see how easy it is for a country to get to this situation.

Breakeven

This situation arises when a country is spending exactly the amount it is earning on an on-going basis, as we read earlier in the BREAKEVEN chapter. Jennifer's story shows us how this is quite dangerous as it allows no room for unexpected costs, which we know are a normal part of life. It is the same for countries. Eventually, if a country continues like this, it will find itself on the pathway to debt. Disasters can occur in many guises: a country can experience a natural disaster like a hurricane or an earthquake. It could experience a year of crop failure due to bad weather, countries reliant on exporting a certain commodity like steel can be affected by a sudden drastic drop in price, perhaps because there is a glut on the market or the demand for steel has gone considerably down. There are so many unexpected crises that can occur which can leave a country in a devastated state if it is only reliant on a breakeven position. I would advise you to watch the business and world news from a new perspective. You will be surprised to realise that many countries find themselves in this position. It is difficult for me to name a county in this exact position, as it is quite easy for a county to move from breakeven to debt (deficit) very quickly. A country in this situation really needs to ask itself 'What is our financial game plan?' and 'Is our financial plan sustainable now and in the future?' Now that you are clued up, try to find out what your country's financial position is and if it is a good one. I am sure you now know what a good plan should look like.

Savings

When I think of countries that save, I think of Singapore and India. Many Asian communities are renowned for their thrifty lifestyle. This is because most of the time they do not have easily available credit facilities, e.g. CREDIT CARDS, loans or OVERDRAFT FACILITIES, that we have in the WESTERN SOCIETY. In many situations, they will have to pay for their medical bills, and/or fund their old age, especially those who live in the rural parts of Asia. We in the western world have either state healthcare or health insurance cover and old-aged pensions to look forward to. In Asia, debt (credit cards, loans etc.) is not as easily available as it is in the West; hence they rely heavily on their savings. In the last few years, a lot of the Asian countries have been experiencing growth while most of the western economies have stagnated. We sometimes hear these countries referred to as the emerging economies. The Asians are now trying to catch up with the West in their lifestyles, houses, cars and latest gadgets. We can only hope that they do not fall into the debt trap the western world has, but that they manage to live within their means and continue saving. We just need to read Sally's story to understand the benefits of savings. Of course, we hope they enjoy the fruits of their labour and definitely do raise their standard of living but not to the extent that they get themselves into senseless debt. This lifestyle has held them in good stead as the rest of the world has suffered some form of consequence, RECESSION or DEPRESSION, because of debt.

Wealth

The countries that come to mind when considering WEALTH and savings are China and Germany. In terms of the amount of money sitting in their RESERVE ACCOUNTS, China is one of the wealthiest economies in the world today. It is actually a lender, rather than a borrower, of money, and lends to many different countries including Europe, America and Great Britain. Using the reserves they have been building for many years they are now buying up investment OPPORTUNITIES around the world, especially in Africa.

Like Adam, China is increasing its wealth, using its money to buy up commodities and other natural resources for its country and people. This is actually quite a good time to buy as the world is in a recession or depression, meaning China is able to pick up these items at good prices.

The standard of living for the Chinese can only increase with all these investment opportunities, leaving China to become one of the world's super powers.

The Chinese have sacrificed a lot over the years and have had to live quite frugally. They are now reaping the rewards of their efforts, the same as Adam. Sometimes, with countries, the time span of these wealth-building mechanisms coming to fruition can take a lot longer – we are talking about DECADES or longer – whereas for an individual, these can happen in as little as a few years.

Key point

I would like to point out the information contained in this chapter regarding the different countries mentioned are subject to change. We live in a fast-paced world and, as I said previously, a country's situation can change from the time of my writing this book, to publishing it and you reading it. The main emphasis is that you understand the logic being portrayed.

Countries' economies

From the analysis of all four categories, we can clearly see, as with individuals, it is imperative that countries live within their means because eventually debt catches up with us all, as it has Britain and Greece. The debt is still catching up with many countries, America, Spain, Portugal and Italy, and it will be the people of these countries who bear the brunt of this burden – you and me.

Therefore, it is important that we the people have an understanding of the way our country's finances are handled, because this does impact on us. Not just us and our current families, but our children and their children. All will be affected, including the future generations.

I would also like to point out that we are now in the age of **DELEVERAGING**.

> **DELEVERAGING**
>
> For those of you who have not heard the term deleveraging, it means the paying back of debt by a country, business or individual.

Deleveraging normally takes place when a country, business or individual borrows significantly more than they should. This debt then becomes unsustainable, leading to drastic measures taken in the future to reduce this debt. This is what we are currently seeing happening in most western societies, with our respective countries, in our businesses and for us personally. As a society we are now clearing our debts, some more drastically than others. If we do not do this deleveraging exercise then there may be dire consequences to pay in the future, as we saw with Brad.

CHAPTER SUMMARY

Debt, breakeven, savings and wealth lessons for individuals are the same lessons that can be applied to countries. Countries EARN income and have expenses. Their INCOME can come from many different sources, including the one we are all familiar with: TAXES. A country also has EXPENSES it has to pay out, like teachers and police officers' salaries.

When a country's income is more than its expenses that country is operating a **SURPLUS** or what we term SAVINGS.

If a country's expenses are more than its income then that country is operating a **DEFICIT** or what we call DEBT.

All deficit or debt needs to be repaid using the exact same principle as individuals. Countries do not have special privileges. They too need to repay their debts.

Countries in debt apply government cuts in different areas of their society. That government needs to raise money somehow to pay their debts and reducing its costs in one area means it can pay off the debt in another area.

It is important that we as individuals have an understanding of the way our country's finances are handled because it impacts upon us, our friends and family, and future generations; our children and their children.

RISE OF THE CONSUMER
History Revisited

A thirty to forty year time span

Why did I feel the need to write this chapter? I believe it will enlighten many people who may not understand how dramatically lifestyles have changed over the last few DECADES. I know this chapter will be a great eye opener for a lot of people.

I felt it necessary to go back into history of how our own lifestyle has changed compared to our parents' and grandparents'. I must stress that this exploration is based on the western society, which encompasses Europe, America and

Great Britain and other FIRST WORLD COUNTRIES, and may not necessarily apply to Asia and Africa and other THIRD WORLD COUNTRIES today.

One of the key factors leading to this change in lifestyle within the western society was greater introduction of CREDIT, otherwise known as DEBT, into a country and into the lifestyle of the individuals in that country. These increases in credit facilities were due to **mainly** three reasons:

1. A more lax approach by banks and lending institutions with their lending criteria. Compared to the guidelines used in the past, which tended to be quite strict, these criteria became more lenient over time. Therefore, it was not an overnight introduction of sometimes careless lending. Borrowing money from these institutions became much easier with passing decades and has now reached a climax in the current decade.

2. Over the last few decades, the various governments have helped by having more lenient regulations for the banks and building societies concerning lending and the availability of credit to the general public. Again this was a gradual process over a number of years. These governments also assisted by helping to keep INTEREST RATES low and this therefore ensured that borrowing money from lending institutions was not expensive but suddenly affordable or even cheap for individuals and families.

3. We, the individual or family, helped the situation by taking out the now affordable credit facility offered by the banks with their lax criteria that the government approved through their lenient regulations. This also was a process that grew significantly, creating a DEBT CULTURE, affecting too many people.

People would have started off being wary of debt back in the 70s and early 80s. In the 90s it became easier to get a LOAN or MORTGAGE, and debt became more acceptable. When we reached the start of the last decade, debt had become very common and very accessible. It started out with individuals putting their feet in the shallow waters, starting with small controllable debt, which then grew continuously through the decades until people were deep in the ocean trying to stay above water. The debt culture was now way out of control, and people found themselves in the same situation as Brad, sinking in the ocean of debt.

Looking at this, we can get an idea that we all played a part in this move from a savings culture to a debt culture. It was not just the banks and lending institutions, and the government, but also us, the individual. We will look at SAVINGS and spending habits over roughly thirty to forty years to show you how we as a society have moved from a lifestyle of savings and prudence to one of debt and extravagance. As we read in the earlier chapters with Brad and Jennifer, this new lifestyle has affected our lives, our families and even our health.

157

Roughly, thirty to forty years ago our parents and grandparents had a simpler lifestyle. They tended to live within their means and generally did not have debt to their name unless it was through one of the traditional methods: a mortgage, small loan or HIRE PURCHASE. (Hire purchase is a method of buying goods through making installment payments over time. Under a hire purchase contract, the buyer is leasing the goods and does not obtain ownership until the full amount of the contract is paid.) The availability of debt was not easy as it is today. Sally's savings principle, which we read about earlier, would have been the common practice back then.

Let's take a look at how debt has evolved:

LOAN

A loan is defined as the temporary provision of money (usually to be paid back with INTEREST).

A BANK LOAN is a loan made by a bank, to be repaid with interest on or before a fixed date.

Getting a loan twenty to thirty years ago was not as easy as it is today. The criteria for a loan back in the 60s, 70s, and the 80s was very strict, and even in the 90s, where the lending rules were more lax, it still was not easy to get a loan. Therefore not many people applied because they knew their circumstances were not right and they would be turned down. The banks tended to have strict guidelines that they would follow before a person could qualify for a loan and it was a much longer process to apply than it is today, lasting from one week to even a few months before a loan would be approved and the money paid into the person's bank account. Today we can pick up a phone and ring our bank and have the loan approved within the same day, with access to the loan money within a few days if not the next day. We can even apply for a loan via the internet and have instant approval.

Loans back in the 70s and 80s would have been more expensive for an individual because of higher interest rates than we have today. For example in the 80s loan interest rates in Britain went up to, on average, 16%. In this current period average interest rates are 8%. Therefore the monthly repayment for an individual in the 80s would have been more expensive. Many people stayed away from loans for this very reason.

In the 70s and 80s when a person took out a loan they would have to give the specific reason for needing the money and these had to be valid and necessary reasons; they needed the money to sort out an issue or a problem or even to start a business. Things are totally different today. Yes, a lot of us do take out loans for valid reasons, but some of us simply take out loans because we can, without knowing why we need it. As loan facilities are so easily available, we are tempted to take up what seems like a great opportunity. Loans come in many different forms and do not necessarily have to come from the traditional institution, the bank. These days we have a rise in online loan companies where you do not even have to talk to someone, making it even easier than going into banks to apply for and get a loan. So as you can see, cheap loans, lenient lending criteria, and changing reasons why we need to take out a loan have definitely evolved over the last thirty to forty years.

CREDIT CARDS

A credit card is a small plastic card issued to individuals as a system of payment. It allows people who have a card to buy goods and services based on that person's promise to pay for these goods and services in the future.

In the 60s and 70s, credit cards were less well known and only used by a few categories of people, mainly business people or company employees and the rich. It was not the phenomenon it is today where they are easily accessible to one and all. Today, everyone can apply for one: young and old, students, the retired and even the unemployed. Credit cards are now common and most individuals over the age of eighteen will have had a credit card at some point in their lives. A credit card is a promise to pay later for goods and services we buy now. It is credit that we spend that will need to be paid back one day. Credit cards are one of the easiest forms of getting credit that individuals can apply for and get approved.

For this very reason, credit cards are very dangerous because the majority of the time we get a credit card with no purpose in mind for it. We do not usually have a specific use for it as we do when we take out a loan, and I have known of people scratching their heads after maxing out their CREDIT LIMIT on their card wondering what they spent their money on. They are a real HIDDEN TRAP and a person must be careful if they own one because it is so easy to use and tempting to put items on the card for payment later. Credit cards have definitely made it easier to spend money we do not have for items we want or need now without having to worry about how to pay it back until a future time.

OVERDRAFT FACILITY

An overdraft facility is a prior agreement with the bank or account provider for an agreed amount to be withdrawn below the zero balance.

An overdraft occurs when money is withdrawn from a bank account and the available balance goes below zero. In this situation, the account is said to be 'overdrawn'.

As we read about with credit cards above, overdraft facilities are not a new thing, but they were not as easily and readily available to the general public as they have been for the last two decades. An overdraft is basically a loan, but one that is not as structured or formal. You do not need to have a standard repayment policy and, depending on if you meet your bank's criteria, you can re-negotiate and extend the overdraft time and limit.

Again, an overdraft can be as dangerous as a credit card because it is so readily available and sometimes you are not even aware you have gone into this facility until you look at your bank statement.

As I mentioned above, this phenomenon has grown within the last two decades. Many of our grandparents did not even have a bank account, let alone an overdraft facility. They had no option but to spend only the money they had available to them. This was their INCOME or salary, not an overdraft facility and not a credit card. Therefore, even if they needed basic necessities but had no cash they would have to do without.

MORTGAGES

A mortgage is a loan secured against a property (usually a house) to be repaid within a set period, normally twenty to thirty years.

Even as late as the 60s and early 70s, many families rented the place in which they lived in. Mortgages were very expensive and families needed large DEPOSITS in order even to be considered for this loan. It was not the norm for families to have their own home or a mortgage unless the home had been inherited from their parents or grandparents.

Within the last three decades, there has been a more lenient approach to mortgage applications. Both the government and the banks have worked together to make mortgages more accessible and cheaper to the general public. Even though the concept and idea of families owning their own home is a good thing, this leniency in the mortgage criteria has been detrimental for many families. A large number of families have taken out mortgages and later found themselves in debt situations that they are unable to handle or cope with. I believe that it was a good vision by both the bank and the government to want families to own their own homes, but the leniency introduced to the guidelines and criteria was too lax compared to the criteria used in the 70s and 80s. Under these laxer rules, many families took out mortgages they could not afford and so the debt culture grew.

Three major ways leniency was introduced to mortgage lending, making it easier for individuals and families to get mortgages, were 1) INTEREST-ONLY MORTGAGES (a type of mortgage in which the person is only required to pay off the interest that arises from the mortgage money borrowed), 2) cheaper mortgages and 3) a smaller deposit needed as down-payment for a property. This was detrimental for many families who could not afford them, leading to the rise in repossessions of houses for many, or families taking on larger amounts of debt to cover their living expenses because their mortgages were too expensive.

Lifestyle changes evolution

To get a true perspective when writing this section I had to draw on the knowledge of my older friends and colleagues, and their views were quite a revelation for me. I have included some of their viewpoints.

1. Fashion industry

I start with fashion as this is one of the major industries in the world today, bringing in billions yearly to this market. We seem to be a society consumed with fashion, having to have the latest trends in clothing, shoes, handbags, jewellery, makeup, perfume and much more. We have television advertisements promoting fashion, we have bill boards on most major street corners promoting fashion, we have magazines dedicated to fashion, we have cat walk shows and designers launching new trends, the 'must haves' of the new season. The window displays of our high street stores are continuously updated to show the latest designer trends. This trend is ever changing and it only takes a few months from the time of launching an item to that item being out of season. I know this very well because I used to be consumed by the fashion industry, putting myself under financial pressure to keep up with the trend. After a while, it can become an addiction, keeping up with the latest fashion, because we as a society are bombarded daily with it. This is the power the industry has over us. I am sure what I am saying is resonating with quite a few if not all of you. Yet thirty years ago we did not have such intense fashion marketing bombarding us from every direction. Today, fashion marketing is big business with huge amounts of money spent to entice us to spend.

Some of us have become shopping addicts, feeling a need to go shopping every few days regardless of what our finances look like. We are taught to believe that shopping is a stress buster, relieving the stress of work or home life, not realising that shopping can sometimes be the cause of this stress. Our minds are programmed by the images we see every day in advertisements, magazines and fashion shows. This bombardment has been going on for the last few decades. We are programmed to view fashions and the latest trends as ASSETS, something that will help us land the dream job, make us feel good, or attract the perfect husband or wife. Therefore, we believe, we must spend money on these so-called must-have 'assets'.

Wow, how times have changed! From the 60s, fashion has become increasingly more important. However, it seems to have taken off into a new level from the 90s until now in the current decade. Fashion has caused quite a few of us to get into debt trying to look good by keeping up with the latest trend. I remember not too long ago, about fifteen or twenty years ago, that this was not the case. People did spend money on clothes but the fashion trends were not so fast changing.

Back then, there were not as many fashion or designer stores and many people bought clothes for their practicality, not just for their looks. Many mums would have owned a sewing machine and either made or mended clothes for members of the family, which usually worked out to be much cheaper than buying them. There were a lot more fabric stores then. Today it is much easier and much cheaper to buy rather than make clothes

The fashion world of late has become such a whirlwind and I hope a lot of us wise up to this fact and do not fall in the trap of keeping up with appearances.

2. The introduction and rise of technology in the home

We now live in homes full of technology. We have new or improved technology in practically every room in the home. As with the fashion industry, the home technology and gadgets arena is a billion dollar industry, raking in money with the continuous introduction or improvement of gadgets. We have become gadget crazy, spending without thinking of the cost because these items have become 'must have', 'can't live without' items, or so we have been programmed to think. Fewer and fewer homes have not kept up with this rise in technology. Most homes can be technologically savvy everywhere, from the garage with its automatic doors to the security system in homes. The kitchen has so many electric gadgets that it can get confusing keeping up with them. Let us not even go near the living/TV room area where we spend most of our time! This room can cost a fortune kitting out.

Technology has moved very quickly in the last decade or two and has swept into our lives like a storm. Every item coming onto the market is being advertised as the next best thing since slice bread, encouraging us to spend money. It has consumed us and massively changed our lives, sometimes not for the best. Electricity bills are definitely much more expensive than they were in the 60s, 70s and 80s.

Most of these items did not exist in the 60s and 70s; a few were introduced in the 1980s. Some of our parents or grandparents have not even heard of these gadgets and can sometimes find them very confusing, for example, the computer, which is now a common part of everyday life for most of us. This was not so in the 60s, 70s or even 80s where it was practically non-existent in the home. Homes and families during this time did not have the pressure of spending quite a large portion of their salaries on these so-called must-have technologies that today can cost a fortune.

Yes, improved, innovative and new technology is great, but not at the cost of escalating our spending to new and higher levels trying to keep up in this ever-moving fast-paced industry. Gadgets and their costs were so much simpler 'back in the day'!

3. Holidays

Holidays in the 70s and 80s tended to be basic. Even flying abroad for a holiday was a thing a family would do once every two to three years if at all; it was definitely not the way it is today. Today it is quite common and almost expected that we take a holiday abroad at least once a year, some people even take four or five holidays within that year period. If you can afford to take a holiday a year then by all means do. However, there are too many people who cannot afford to, yet still go on holiday because 'it is expected and everyone does it'. And how is this cost paid for? Usually with a credit card or by using an overdraft.

4. Buying a home

As discussed previously today we see many young, newlywed couples buying their home as soon as they get married. Many single, young people take on a mortgage because it is the 'in thing' to have your own home. We must remember that a mortgage is a huge financial commitment, if not the biggest one most families take on.

This did not use to be the case thirty years ago. Most young families or newlyweds would rent or live with family members and save money for a few years before purchasing a home. Buying a home was not common unless you had saved up quite a deposit, and the bank had strict guidelines you had to meet before they would agree to give a mortgage for a home. If a family could not afford a house then they could not get a mortgage from the bank, it was as simple as that. They would be refused and the family would rent a house until they could afford to buy one, if they could not, they would rent for life.

5. Weddings

In today's society expensive and grand weddings have become the expected practice; a must have. This is vastly different to our parents' and grandparents' time where a wedding was a cause for great celebration but was also affordable. A wedding then would be held in the local community hall or in the family house. Today we see the rise of luxurious venues as *the* place to have your wedding and these venues do not come cheap. Add to that the cost of the wedding dress and the increasingly expected weekend away for the hen night or stag do and we are finding that weddings are costing an enormous amount.

What has caused this change? The access of easy money or debt has allowed many couples, both young and old, to have extravagant weddings they cannot afford through the use of credit cards, overdraft and loans. It is quite common these days to pay for a wedding with debt and sort the bill out in the future. Hence newlywed couples are starting their lives together with debt they cannot afford. A stressful way to start their new lives together!

The rise of the expensive exotic honeymoon, which can sometimes cost a fortune, is also quite common today. This is totally different to the way previous generations lived. Some of them did not even take a honeymoon for the plain fact that they could not afford it, or they would save up for several years and take the honeymoon when they had sufficient money. It can be very surprising, given today's climate, if we ask our parents or grandparents 'did they take a honeymoon?' that their answer is 'NO'.

6. Baby industry

How excited people can get when they realise they are having a much-wanted baby. Although it is great news with wonderful emotions, today the preparation and cost of having a baby is completely different to older generations of parents expecting their babies. Having a baby was not quite as costly a process for previous generations. The items needed to raise a baby were quite minimal and did not cost a small fortune. Families often practiced the 'hand-me-down' system where second-hand baby stuff was quite common to use and not frowned upon as it seems to be today.

We now have the rise of the so-called 'baby industry' today. The baby accessories business is booming, and can cost a hefty amount if families are not careful or they fall for the belief that they need all the paraphernalia that bombards them. They need the stroller, the pram, car seat, the baby monitor, even the baby bag can be expensive, the baby sling, the cot/crib, the travel cot... There is this and that, and this and that, when in truth do we really need all this stuff for the baby? Also, more critically, do we need to buy the prestigious brands when they are way too expensive for some of us? Babies are fast growers and some of the items, which we can pay hundreds of pounds for, are only used for a few short months.

7. Home redecoration

Redecorating our home every two to three years or having a constant interior uplift is quite common today. We are continually keeping up with the latest colours and trends, and this costs money. DIY (Do It Yourself) is big business today and we have seen more and more of the big DIY superstores emerge in the last decade or two, making it even easier for individuals to buy materials they need to renovate their homes. We are spending fortunes making our houses look the part, sometimes even redecorating when the old was good enough and could have lasted a few more years, it was just not up-to-date or fashionable. What a potential waste of money!

If we were to visit our grandparents' and even some of our parents' homes, we can see the big difference in comparison to our own homes. They may have had the same interior in their homes for the last ten to twenty years where we have redecorated our homes at least twice in the last ten years.

8. Household spending

Our household spending is much more complicated now than it was a few decades ago. A household back then would have about three or four main bill items they would pay monthly e.g. electricity, water, landline phone, and rent or mortgage.

Today our list of bills is so much more. We have the ones mentioned above (electricity, water, phone, and rent or mortgage) and on top of that we now have mobile phone bills, internet bills, cable television bills, gym membership bills, bills for two cars instead of one, credit card bills, insurance bills... These of course are the most common ones, the list can go on.

Regular eating out and frequently buying takeaway food, instead of the traditional home cooking is definitely a common trend in today's lifestyle. Some of our older grandparents frown upon this type of living as they believe in home cooking being cheaper and more nutritious.

Full spa treatments, manicures, pedicures, facials and massages are also on the rise and are seen as a necessity rather than a luxury in this current day and age. We are definitely in the new age of pampering.

There are still lots more I could have put in to demonstrate how our society has developed into a CONSUMERIST one, but I think you must have the picture and now understand how the trends have changed. Yes, I do believe change is good, and yes, our lifestyle has evolved over time with some of these changes being quite good especially with the busy lifestyle a lot of us live today. However, some of these changes I have mentioned have been to our detriment, especially to those individuals who have not handled their finances wisely. Some have used these changes to their advantage while others have been sucked into the system of debt.

As I mentioned, it is only recently have we seen the increase in credit facility, and it wasn't until the 80s that it really started to show itself, and over the last two decades it has exploded into a phenomenon we have now. The increase of this credit led people to live illusionary lifestyles of perceived WEALTH built on debt. We in the western world have many material things, nice homes, nice cars and all the latest gadgets and fashion, but a lot of this is an illusion built on debt. We only have to take a look at Brad's story to understand this picture. The sad truth is that quite a large percentage of people are in the same situation as Brad today.

Therefore we can see a big shift over the past forty years to today. Around thirty years ago we only bought things we could afford, or we saved for an item and purchased it with cash or sometimes on hire purchase. Families stuck within their means and if they could not afford a certain thing then they just did not get it. They could not get it because the funding (credit) was not available.

Today we buy the item with a loan or credit card and worry about how to pay for it later.

If you consider your grandparents, or even your parents (depending on your age), some of them did not have the availability of credit; they may not have even heard the term credit card or overdraft in the 70s and early 80s. Therefore the 'buy now, pay later' mentality was not part of their thinking.

CHAPTER SUMMARY

Over the last few decades there have been many changes in our lifestyles and spending habits. These changes include us as individuals, businesses and governments taking on more DEBT and spending more as the DECADES have progressed.

The introduction of new methods of debt, like **CREDIT CARDS** and **OVERDRAFT FACILITIES**, has greatly assisted us in becoming a CONSUMERIST society in the **'western world'**.

We should ask ourselves how we can change our current habits after reading the information in this chapter. We looked at many different areas including fashion, technology, weddings and many others. How have these areas affected us and what can we do to improve them?

Conclusion
Where do we go from here?

I hope you have enjoyed meeting our four friends and learning about their different financial approaches. Brad and Adam's stories are what I call the extreme ends of their spectrum. Jennifer and Sally's stories on the other hand are in the middle ground and what most of us can relate to.

A few of you may have thought Adam's story unattainable, possibly due to your age or your current financial position. Yes, Adam's story was at the extreme end of the scale, but again my aim in this endeavour was to get you thinking about a wealth-making plan, which includes INVESTMENT. Please do not let your present financial situation or age dictate to you where you will be in five or ten years' time. You should set your financial future and try not to let society or circumstances set it for you, even though they might try to.

I used one of the worst possible case scenarios for Brad to paint a true picture about the consequences of DEBT. However, many people fall into different levels of debt and not necessarily at Brad's excessive end. I know some of you may have found Brad's story a harsh reality. I have personally known a few people who have been in this situation and seen the stress they have been through because of it. Especially with the current economical environment we live in, many have been made redundant and many are still being affected by the current climate. People are taking on debt sometimes because they simply have to survive.

We have lived in a DEBT CULTURE for the last ten to twenty years. However, I believe the system is now reversing and we are coming into a new phase in our lifestyles and culture in the WESTERN SOCIETY. This shift started when the stock market crashed with the banking crisis of 2008/2009, and we are now slowly adapting to a new lifestyle or the beginning of a new culture; what I call 'the DELEVERAGING culture'. I briefly touched on this in the *Global Analysis* chapter. Deleveraging is a word we are hearing very often these days, on the television, from our politicians, and in our newspapers. As a reminder deleveraging means the reduction of debt in a household, business or country.

We are now in the new DECADE of payback time. There will be a lot of changes over this next decade. Unlike previously, where we had access to easy CREDIT, it will no longer be so simple to acquire. MORTGAGES, LOANS, CREDIT CARDS and OVERDRAFT FACILITIES now have stricter guidelines and are not as easily available as in the last decade.

Households will have to pay back the debts they have. As we read in Brad's story, there is still hope and Brad took the bull by the horns and decided to handle his finances wisely, even though he was late in the game compared to his colleagues, Sally and Adam. This book is intended for you to really gain wisdom in personal financial planning. By reading this book I hope you will go away with a host of knowledge and an understanding of how money can work for you or against you, and how society helps in forming the culture we live in, be it good or bad.

I am of the opinion that if we have knowledge then we should learn from this knowledge and apply it to our lives. I do hope this is what you will do. I trust the majority of you reading this book will thrive with this new ammunition you have for making a success of your personal finances. I personally believe prevention is better than cure, and hope that you will learn this concept through the lives of the characters Brad, Jennifer, Sally and Adam.

Closing Thought

A final thought before I close off this book and something that I need to say to you. There are times when circumstances occur that are way beyond our control, and no ONE-OFF EXPENSE FUND or SAVINGS FUND can stop us getting into a debt situation. It could be because of medical reasons, redundancy, a death in the family or any other situations that can lead to us having no choice but to take on an amount of debt with the hope that fortunes will change in the future. This can happen to anyone, even to those who are excellent with finances. These are sometimes unfortunate circumstances but again these are extreme cases and I want to say for those individuals who find themselves in this position I sympathise and I understand that these situations do occur. Regardless of this, I do believe you must still be wise with your finances even though it seems beyond your control and even hopeless. Good financial stewardship will always hold you in good stead, and though it may mean nothing to you right now reading this book, there is always HOPE.

If you enjoyed this book, please look out for the next installment of the 'Brad & Adam' series by

Neala Okuromade

Coming Soon

Brad & Adam Series, Book 2:

WHAT'S YOUR INVESTMENT GAME PLAN?

Wondered how Adam created his wealth, what he did and how he went about it?

Discover the same practical insights and principles as Book 1 *What's Your Financial Game Plan*, but now we will be looking at investment. Neala will be debunking Adam's wealth creation story, making it accessible, uncomplicated and understandable for the everyday person.

If you have never thought of an investment strategy or don't know how or where to start to invest in today's volatile economic climate then this is the book for you.

Some of the things this book will take you through are:

- Investing in stocks and shares
- The property market
- Currencies
- Investing in a business
- The mystery of gold and silver
- Pensions

Other topics include; Should I diversify my investments? How much money should I have invested in each section?

Simple and Easy is the Motto of this book but with investment tips and advice you never would have thought about.

This book will help answer these questions and equip you to be WISE and sensible investors in this ever changing economic environment.

Please note this book isn't about getting rich quick but how to invest for the long term and see your money grow over time using a variety of different approaches including having a fool proof investment plan.

www.bradandadamseries.com

Glossary

Asset Any item of 'economic value' owned by an individual, company or government; especially that which could be converted to cash. Examples are cash, property, car, and stocks and shares.

Bank Loan *see* LOANS

Bankruptcy The legal process whereby a person declares their inability to pay their DEBTS. Upon a court declaration, a person surrenders their ASSETS (i.e. house, car etc.) and is relieved from the payment of previous debts. In the U.S. and U.K., this status is established through legal procedures involving a petition by the bankrupt person or entity, or by its creditors.

Blacklisted A person under suspicion, considered untrustworthy, disloyal, to be boycotted or penalised especially by a government or an organisation. In the context of this book, it is the person's inability or unwillingness to pay their obligations which leads to their name being blacklisted.

Bonus Something given or paid in addition to what is usual or expected. It is often a sum of money or an equivalent given to an employee in addition to the employee's usual salary or compensation.

Breakeven   In general, the point at which gains equal losses. For this book, breakeven is when monthly INCOME equals monthly EXPENSES, or when a country is spending exactly the amount it is earning on an on-going basis.

Budget   An estimation of our INCOME and EXPENSES over a specified future period of time. A budget can be made for a person, family, business, government or country. Budgets are usually compiled and re-evaluated periodically and adjustments are made to budgets based on the goals of the budgeting person, country or organisation.

Car Cost   For the context of this book, car cost is all the costs necessary for running and maintaining a car. These costs cover car payment, insurance, TAXES, fuel and maintenance costs.

Cash Flow   *see* SAVINGS

Compounding   *see* DEBT COMPOUNDING and WEALTH COMPOUNDING.

Consumerist   A person who gives too much attention to buying and owning things, often things that are not really necessary.

Court Judgment   *see* Financial Court Judgment

Credit   An arrangement between a financial institution, usually a bank, and a customer that establishes a maximum LOAN balance that the bank will permit the borrower to maintain. The borrower can draw down on the line of credit at any time, as long as he or she does not exceed the maximum set in the agreement.

Credit Cards   A small plastic card issued to individuals as a system of payment. It allows people who have a card to buy goods and services now, and requires that person to pay for these goods and services in the future, usually with interest (*see* INTEREST RATES). Some stores issue cards for purchase of their goods and services. These are known as Store Cards.

Credit History or **Credit Report**   A record of an individual's past borrowing and repayments, including information about late payments and BANKRUPTCY.

Credit Limit   The maximum amount of CREDIT that a bank or other lender will extend to a customer, or the maximum that a CREDIT CARD company will allow a card holder to borrow on a single card.

Credit Score (or Credit Rating)   A credit score represents the creditworthiness of that person. Lenders use credit scores to determine who qualifies for a LOAN, at what INTEREST RATE, and what CREDIT LIMITS.

Debt   An obligation or liability to pay or render something, usually money, to someone else. If an individual spends more than they earn then after a while they will accumulate debt and this always needs to be repaid. They may need to

185

pay back a bank, building society, family or friend, but the money will need to be paid back depending on the terms and conditions negotiated.

Debt Compounding   When debt burden becomes so large it inevitably begins to progressively increase interest payments leading to greater debt. (Interest upon interest.)

Debt Culture   Each time a lender struck a deal with a borrower, it reinforced a new definition of acceptable behaviour for society. Over the last two decades the normalising of acquiring debt has lead people to live illusionary lifestyles of perceived WEALTH built on DEBT. We in the western world have many material things; but a lot of this is an illusion.

Decade   A period of ten years. An example of decade is 2001 to 2010. Although any period of ten years is a decade, a convenient and frequently referenced interval is based on the tens digit of a calendar year, as in using '1990s' or '90s' to represent the decade from 1990 to 1999.

Deficit   In economics, a deficit is a shortfall in revenue, a DEBT. In more specific cases it may refer to, for example, a trade deficit, when the value of imports exceed the value of exports in a country.

Deleverage   This is the reduction of DEBT in a household, business or country.

Deposit A sum payable as a first installment on the purchase of something or as a pledge for a contract, the balance being payable later: The one we are familiar with is a deposit paid for a house.

Depression A severe and prolonged RECESSION characterised by falling price levels, inefficient economic productivity in goods and services, and high unemployment. The economy begins to shut down.

Disbursement The act of paying out or disbursing money. Disbursements can include money paid out to run a business, spending cash and grant payments.

Earnings[1] (in relation to an office or employment) any salary, wage or fee or any other profit or incidental benefit of any kind obtained by an employee in return for services given

Earnings[2] The amount of profit that a company produces during a specific period, which is usually defined as a quarter or a year. Earnings typically refer to after-TAX net income.

Envelope System Where an individual puts a set amount of money aside on a month by month basis for certain categories like food, shopping, eating out and other miscellaneous items.

Expense (expenditure)   An outflow of money to another person or group to pay for an item or service, or for a category of costs. Buying food, clothing, furniture or an automobile is often referred to as an expense. An expense is a cost that is "paid", usually in exchange for something of value.

Exponentially   describes a rate of increase that is extremely quick, appearing to grow rapidly

Finance Counsellor   A person whose job is to give financial advice and help to people so they can manage their income and expenses, including debt, more successfully

Financial Advisor   A professional who provides financial advice or guidance to customers for compensation. Financial advisors can provide many different services, such as investment management, income tax preparation and estate planning.

Financial Court Judgment (also known as a County Court Judgment)   For the context of this book this is a legal decision handed down by Courts in different countries that has a very negative impact on a person's CREDIT RATING and make it nearly impossible for that individual to gain any form of regular CREDIT or finance for a period of time, unless the judgment is set aside, or the amount outstanding is paid in full.

Financial Investment Vehicles Financial instruments whose value is determined directly by the financial markets. These vehicles can include investing in the stock market e.g. via shares, bonds, ETF's (exchange traded funds) or unit trusts.

Financial Plan A series of steps or goals used by an individual to accomplish a final financial goal or set of goals, e.g. elimination of DEBT, early repayment of a MORTGAGE, etc.

Financial Statement *see* INCOME AND EXPENDITURE STATEMENT.

First World Countries So-called developed, capitalist, industrial countries; a bloc of countries with more or less common political and economic interests. Examples include North America, Western Europe, Japan and Australia. *see also* THIRD WORLD COUNTRIES

Fixed Rule Approach In the context of this book the 'fixed rule approach' is when you apply a fixed monetary amount as an expense to your monthly income, e.g. saving £50 every month.

Fun and Entertainment All the costs associated within the spreadsheets listed in this book under 'fun and entertainment', e.g. dining out, going to the cinema or theme park and any other cost that may fall into this category that is specific to the characters in this book or you.

Grants   Are non-repayable funds given by one party, often a government department, corporation, foundation or trust, to a recipient, often an educational institution, business or an individual.

Hidden Trap   An individual not aware or not budgeting for one-off expenses, like a fridge needing to be fixed or the purchase of a birthday present. The person is under the illusion that their total monthly bills are covered. These situations not planned for then leads the individual into unnecessary DEBT.

High-Risk Investment   INVESTMENTS that involve a greater than usual amount of risk when investing. A fundamental idea in finance is the relationship between RISK and return. The greater the amount of risk that an investor is willing to take on, the greater the potential return. The reasoning for this is that investors need to be compensated for taking on additional risk. *see also* INVESTMENT

Hire Purchase   A method of buying goods through making installment payments over time. Under a hire purchase contract, the buyer leases the goods and does not obtain ownership until the full amount of the contract is paid.

Income   The flow of cash or cash-equivalents received from work (wage or salary), capital (interest or profit), or land (rent).

Income and Expenditure Statement (also referred to in this book as a Financial Statement)   A statement to measure an individual's financial performance over a specific period of time. A person's financial performance is assessed by giving a summary of how that person incurs their income and expenses. It also shows the profit or loss incurred over a specific period, typically a month, quarter or year

Interest   *see* INTEREST RATES

Interest-Only Mortgage   A type of MORTGAGE where a person is only required to pay off the INTEREST that arises from the mortgage money borrowed, leaving the capital still owing.

Interest Rates   The rate charged or paid for using money. You are charged an interest rate (payment on top of the amount) when you borrow money and paid an interest rate when you loan money (an amount on top of the loan amount). Placing money in a SAVINGS FUND or INVESTMENT FUND is like a loan to the bank, so you are paid interest on your savings. With CREDIT CARDS, LOANS and MORTGAGES the interest rate directly influences the cost of borrowing. Lower interest rates mean you'll pay a lower cost (for example 5% of your DEBT), while higher interest rates mean a higher cost (for example 18% of your debt).

Investment   Putting money into FINANCIAL or NON-FINANCIAL VEHICLE or instrument that has some degree of RISK, in the hope of seeing the money grow significantly over time. *see also* HIGH-RISK INVESTMENT and LOW-RISK INVESTMENT

Investment Fund For the context of this book it is a fund used solely and specifically for investing. An individual puts money aside from their salary into this fund until they are ready to invest.

Investment Vehicle Any method that individuals or businesses can invest in and, ideally, grow their money. There is a wide variety of investment vehicles and many investors choose to hold at least several types in their portfolios. *see also* FINANCIAL INVESTMENT VEHICLE and NON-FINANCIAL INVESTMENT VEHICLE.

Liability An obligation that legally binds an individual, company or government to settle a DEBT. When one is liable for a debt, they are responsible for paying the debt.

Loans The temporary provision of money (usually at interest); a bank loan – a loan made by a bank; to be repaid with interest on or before a fixed date.

Loans and Credit Cards A heading in the spreadsheets of this book that represents the monthly payments Brad, Jennifer or an individual pays towards clearing his debt balance. DEBT balance is made up of all loans excluding MORTGAGES, all CREDIT CARDS and STORE CARDS and any PAYDAY LOANS one may have.

Low-Risk Investment INVESTMENTS that are likely to be successful, or unlikely to be connected with danger or problems. Returns are unlikely to deviate from expectations. The main reason individuals buy low-risk investments is because there is a very small chance that they will lose capital. *see also* INVESTMENT.

Mortgages A LOAN secured against a property (usually a house) to be repaid within or by a set period of time, normally twenty to thirty years. *see also* RE-MORTGAGE

Non-Financial Investment Vehicle INVESTMENTS that do not deal with financial or investment-related goods or services that individuals or businesses can invest in and, ideally, grow their money. These can include running your own small business, INVESTING in an already existing business or investing in property, either commercial or residential.

One-Off Expenses Costs that occur in our day-to-day lives. It covers EXPENSES of items that would eventually need to be replaced or fixed for example kettle, iron and blender. It includes gifts for birthdays, weddings, anniversaries, also small emergency bills and many other situations that crop up day-to-day.

One-Off Expense Fund Otherwise known as a Rainy Day Fund. This can be defined as a fund for small, miscellaneous costs that arise in our day-to-day lives.

Opportunities In the context of this book, opportunities are openings, occasions or chances to get involved with a great INVESTMENT. They can be business, stock market or property.

Overdraft Facility When money is withdrawn from a bank account and the available balance goes below zero. In this situation, the account is said to be 'overdrawn'. An overdraft facility is a prior agreement with the bank or account provider for an agreed amount to be withdrawn below the zero balance.

Payday Loans A payday loan is a small, short-term, unsecured LOAN "regardless of whether repayment of loan is linked to a borrower's payday". Payday advance loans rely on the consumer having previous payroll and employment records. Legislation regarding payday loans varies widely between different countries.

Pension A regular payment made during a person's retirement from an investment fund that a person or their employer has contributed to during their working life.

Percentage Rule Approach In the context of this book the 'percentage rule approach' is applying a percentage (%) of your monthly INCOME to an expense like the example used in the savings chapter with Sally saving 10% of her monthly income. *see also* FIXED RULE APPROACH

Rainy Day Fund *see also* ONE-OFF EXPENSE FUND

Recession A period of general economic decline in a country typically accompanied by a drop in the stock market, an increase in unemployment, and a decline in the housing market. A recession is generally considered less severe than a DEPRESSION, although if a recession continues long enough it is often then classified as a depression.

Re-mortgage Paying off an existing MORTGAGE and entering into a new one, usually to obtain a lower rate of interest or a larger loan. This is the process where a mortgage on a property is moved from one lender to another. The new mortgage is used to repay the existing lender and at the same time additional funds may be raised for other purposes.

Reserve Account For the purpose of this book a reserve account is simply a SAVINGS account that a country maintains.

Risk The possibility of being exposed to danger or loss. Financially it is the probability that an actual return on an investment will be lower than the expected return.

Savings Putting money into virtually RISK-free FINANCIAL VEHICLES or instruments where it can grow slowly and safely over time. It is important to understand that saving is not risk taking and brings in little or no return. This money should be put into an INTEREST bearing account or into a unit trust cash fund. This money is not for investing but for safe return over time. Savings can also be referred to as 'Cash flow' in the context of this book.

Saving Fund   Generally a fund available for long-term or short-term goals. It can also exist simply for 'peace of mind'.

Store Cards   *see* CREDIT CARDS

Surplus   A situation in which INCOME exceeds EXPENDITURE, exports exceed imports, or profits exceed losses. A surplus is the opposite of a DEFICIT. When a country exports more than it imports, it is said to have a trade surplus.

Taxes   A means by which governments finance their EXPENDITURE by collecting a contribution from citizens and corporate entities.

Third World Countries   Countries that suffer from low economic development, high levels of poverty, low utilisation of natural resources, and heavy dependence on industrialised nations. *see also* FIRST WORLD COUNTRIES.

Utilities   In the context of this book 'utilities' mentioned in the spreadsheets listed is an everyday necessity cost to the home. Utilities cover water bills, electricity and gas bills, telephone services, and other essentials.

Wealth   Wealth is defined in this book as 'Possessing well-being, happy, comfortable, or having an abundance of valuable possessions or money'. It can be a measure of the value of all of the assets of worth owned by a person, community, company or country.

Wealth Compounding The ability of an asset to generate EARNINGS, which are then reinvested in order to generate their own earnings. In other words, compounding refers to generating earnings from previous earnings such as interest on interest.

Western Society The culture of any country that is part of 'The Western World', and such a country has a European heritage/history. A western country is almost always a democracy, a FIRST WORLD COUNTRY and generally has high living standards with a materialistic and individualistic society. The USA, U.K., France, Canada and Australia are prime examples of Western countries.

Useful Information

For more information on Brad and Adam

Website
www.bradandadamseries.com
Email
neala@bradandadamseries.com

Debt advice centres

Citizens Advice Bureau
http://www.citizensadvice.org.uk

National Debtline
http://www.nationaldebtline.co.uk
Phone: 0808 808 4000

Consumer Credit Counselling Service (CCCS)
http://www.cccs.co.uk
Phone: 0800 138 1111
Wade House
Merrion Centre
Leeds LS2 8NG

Credit report and advice centres

Experian
http://www.experian.co.uk
Phone: 0844 481 0800

Credit Expert
PO Box 7710
Nottingham
NG80 7WE

Equifax
http://www.equifax.co.uk
Equifax Credit File Advice Centre
PO Box 1140
Bradford
BD1 5US

Call Credit
http://www.callcredit.co.uk
Phone: 0845 366 0071
PO Box 491
Leeds LS3 1WZ

check my file
http://www.checkmyfile.com
Phone: 0800 612 0421
Chynoweth House
Trevissome Park
Blackwater
Truro
TR4 8UN

Annual Credit Report
www.annualcreditreport.co.uk

Money bargain and savings websites

Money Saving Expert
http://www.moneysavingexpert.com

Money Supermarket
http://www.moneysupermarket.com

Reading materials

Books
'The Richest Man in Babylon' by George S Clason
'Buffett: The Biography' by Roger Lowenstein

Magazine
Moneywise   http://www.moneywise.co.uk

Index

Fixed Rule Approach   66–8, 69, 120–21
Frugal Lifestyle   *see* Lifestyle – frugal
Fun and Entertainment   47, 51, 115–16
Funds   *see* Investment Fund, One-Off Expense Fund, Savings Fund

Gadgets   *see* Technology
Game Plan   *see* Financial Plan
Get out of Debt   *see* Debt – help for
Gifts   44, 47, 66
Global Economy   141–52, 153
Goal   *see* Financial Goal
Good Debt   4, 31–2, 54, 75–6, 121–6, 127, 131 *see also* Bad Debt, Debt
Government Benefits   *see* Benefits
Government Cuts   145–6, 153

Help   *see* Debt – help for
Hidden Costs   *see* Unexpected Costs
Hidden Traps   35, 38, 42, 45, 161
High Interest Rates   *see* Interest Rates
High-Risk Investment   133–7, 139 *see also* Risk
Hire Purchase   158, 173
Holiday   10–11, 17, 58–60, 62, 88, 94, 124, 167–8
Home Redecoration   170–1
Homework   *see* Research
Honeymoon   9–10, 62, 169 *see also* Wedding
Household Spending   171–2
House Purchase   10, 50, 52–4, 57–8, 75, 114, 119, 163, 168

Illusionary Wealth   17–18, 21, 80–1, 172